Art and the Occult

It is the glory of God to conceal a thing:
but the honour of kings *is* to search out a matter.

The heaven for height, and the earth for depth,
and the heart of kings *is* unsearchable.

Proverbs 25, 2–3

Occult . . . a. . . . 1. Hidden (from sight); concealed.
Now *rare* or *Obs.* 1567 b. Applied to a line drawn in
the construction of a figure but not forming part of the
finished figure; also to a dotted line 1669; 2. Secret;
communicated only to the initiated 1533. 3. Not ap-
prehensible by the mind; recondite, mysterious 1545.
b. Imperceptible by the senses. Now *rare* . . . c. Applied
to physical qualities discoverable only by experiment,
or to those whose nature was unknown and unexplained . . . 4. Of the nature of or pertaining to those
sciences involving the knowledge or use of the supernatural (as magic, alchemy, astrology, theosophy, and
the like); also *transf.* magical, mystical 1663.

The Shorter Oxford English Dictionary

Art and the Occult

PAUL WALDO-SCHWARTZ

George Braziller   New York

Acknowledgments

I wish to thank all those who have graciously helped me
in the gathering of photographic material.

Paris: Galerie Claude Bernard; Galerie Jeanne Bucher;
Le Point Cardinal; Galerie du Dragon; Galerie des Quatres
Directions; Galerie Stadler; Galerie Michel Cachoux;
Galerie J. C. Gaubert; Photos Bulloz; Photos Giraudon.
London: Hugh Moss Ltd.; Nicholas Treadwell Gallery;
Stooshnoff Gallery.
New York: Pace Gallery.

Copyright © 1975 by Paul Waldo-Schwartz

Published simultaneously in Canada by McGraw-Hill Ryerson Ltd.

For information address the publisher:
George Braziller, Inc., One Park Avenue, New York, N.Y. 10016

Library of Congress Catalog Card Number: 75–7655
International Standard Book Number: 0–8076–0784–3, cloth
                                        0–8076–0785–1, paper

Printed in the U.S.A.

DESIGNED BY RONALD FARBER

Contents

Preface and Dedication

The question is asked repeatedly: What is the answer? Yet this is a form of inquiry best suited to detective stories—where the problem is neatly set so that the solution can be ingeniously unraveled. The occult mind works in just the opposite direction. The real concern of the mage—the poet and magician—is: What is the question? That knot has been gnawed at, painted at, written at, and loved at eternally. It is the subject of higher mathematics just as it is the subject of poetry.

This brief book cannot hope to encompass all those who shaped their lives to this intricate and strenuous pursuit; we are dealing here with examples. Many others among the precious few have dived as deep and emerged with remnants as rare. Yet all have been part of the same non-self—the self beyond ego—which never fails to see the "answer" as a tinsel fragment of time, and the question as the medium of time-lessness.

These pages, written in an age besotted with answers, are dedicated to all those so lucid in their innocence as to have sought the question.

Art and the Occult

"Occult revivals" have come about at many periods in modern history, usually for reasons that seem entirely obscure. The collective mind unexpectedly turns from the outer husk of experience which men choose to call reality, the eye turns from material semblance to a sudden inner realization, and the springs of other "realities" are invoked.

The world is now witnessing another such upsurge, but one that differs from its predecessors in dramatic fashion. This one comes at a time of unprecedented pressure; it coincides with a life-and-death struggle to preserve the survival of the planet, to come to grips with bewildering and ever accelerating change, to contain essential energies that can be seen to have gone maverick and lethal.

When, in 1954, Aldous Huxley published *The Doors of Perception*—a book devoted to mind expansion through drugs—it was enthusiastically received. During the same period Zen Buddhism also sprang into vogue as an alternative to the logical processes of Western thought. The world already lived in the shadow of death, but at that time associated the danger with a single perversion of energy—The Bomb. That heresy, monster, and symbol was a clearly silhouetted image of the great enemy, and it could be identified. Some twenty years later the situation has even further deteriorated. The danger of a possible nuclear holocaust now pales slightly in the imagination before prophecies of what survival might entail. Mass pollution, total economic collapse, prevailing anarchy—whose obverse side is totalitarianism—computerized dehumanization, all are possible. The fact imposes itself with horrific certainty that the enemy is no longer without but within.

Significantly, the title of Huxley's book came from William Blake: "If the doors of perception were cleansed, everything will appear to man as it is, infinite." Such was the message of the Buddha, the Prophets, the Christ. Later, the warning and the message came from Blake with amazing prescience. In the eighteenth century he warned against the linear, mechanistic, spiritually emaciated systems of Voltaire, Newton, and Locke. He warned against the desiccating process of the rationalist mind which denied itself and its God— which are in fact one. He insisted that "the eternal body of man is the Imagination, that is, God himself. . . . It manifests itself in his works of art (in Eternity all is vision). Man is all Imagination; God is man and exists in us and we in Him." Thus, Blake saw the full dimensions of what we, so meekly, call the poetic experience:

To see a World in a Grain of Sand
And heaven in a Wild Flower,
Hold Infinity in the palm of your hand
And Eternity in an hour.[1]

In the nuclear age, the natural scientist Loren Eiseley is heard speaking the same message in another "language": "Our identity is a dream. We are process, not reality, for reality is an illusion of the daylight—the light of our particular day." And he observed that "As the spinning, galactic clouds hurl stars and worlds across the night, so life, equally impelled by the centrifugal powers lurking in the germ cell, scatters the splintered radiance of consciousness and sends it prowling and contending through the thickets of the world." [2] There is hope and life and light and vision, but there is no *reality*, in the easy sense.

"Energy," Blake said, "is Eternal Delight." [3] Energy, Albert Einstein agreed, much later, is the preeminent truth ($E=mc^2$) in a world in which all manifestations of that energy are relative. In so saying, he overthrew all the brittle certainties of Newtonian science whose gratifyingly fixed laws were thought to have controlled and explained everything. The "new science" now "proved" Blake correct. It implicitly —but far too late—rendered due homage to the mystics of Asia and of Mexico, who also bowed low before energy and its rhythms. For the machine, once described as "the harnessing of energy to serve man," had long since drained and finally appropriated the powers of the mind. The inner circuits, the internal fire, any true knowledge that makes magic manifest, had been devoured by the dynamo, the electronic circuit, the computer. The processes of the human mind had already been overshadowed by the forces of technology, and a majority of scientists were now supersophisticated plumbers in the employ of the machine.

The magic had fled. Typically, the poet (who, as Blake

realized, is the true realist) grasps the truth before the "realists." This is what Shelley meant when he said, "Poets are the unacknowledged legislators of the world." Through the cataclysm of World War I, the poet-magicians Max Ernst and Marcel Duchamp began to understand the true meaning of the word *alchemy*—not "lead into gold," but "matter into spirit and base spirit into elevated spirit."

As early as 1900, Henry Adams had made the point with prophetic genius. This grandson and great-grandson of American presidents was, unpredictably, a poet disguised as a diplomat. When he arrived in Paris for the *Exposition Universelle*, a showcase of mechanical progress, the scientist-inventor Langley led him to the hall of dynamos. Adams describes his reaction (speaking of himself in the third person):

To him [Langley], the dynamo was but an ingenious channel for conveying somewhere the heat latent in a few tons of poor coal hidden in a dirty enginehouse carefully kept out of sight; but to Adams the dynamo became a symbol of infinity. As he grew accustomed to the great gallery of machines, he began to feel the forty-foot dynamos as a moral force, much as the early Christians felt the Cross. The planet itself seemed less impressive, in its old-fashioned, deliberate, annual or daily revolution, than this huge wheel, revolving within an arm's length at some vertiginous speed, and barely murmuring—scarcely humming an audible warning to stand a hair-breadth further for respect of power—while it would not wake the baby lying close against its frame. Before the end, one began to pray to it; inherited instinct taught the natural expression of man before silent and infinite force. Among the thousand symbols of ultimate energy, the dynamo was not so human as some, but it was the most expressive.[4]

He was able to identify the new forces as "absolute, supersensual, occult." The huge wheel he spoke of had become, to the sorrow of a world Adams would be spared seeing, the spiritual successor to the cosmic circle of the Zodiac, the great Wheel of Buddha, to the wheel in which the Hindu god Siva revolves his cosmic dance, to the infinite Zero of the Tarot, to the great solar and lunar disks so central to biology, magic, and art—as we shall see.

Today these mighty presences and powers are generally ignored. Yet not by all; even through the long reign of rationalist illusion, the artist-magician and certain allies have kept a lucid consciousness alive, have perpetuated a whole-ness of symbols, have preserved a vision possible only along a frequency of truly occult perception, and have seen to it that the converging dignities of art and magic remain united. It "stands to reason" that the members of this unproclaimed league have usually been ignored or persecuted—or only accepted once their works have been formally misunderstood to be objects rather than forces, decorations rather than evocations, rarities of skill rather than emanations of the in-visible, particles of time rather than landmarks of timeless-ness.

In order to approach the nexus of energy and magic which lies at the heart of art and the occult, one must turn to the in-visible.

The In-visible

Speaking for the physical sciences, Sir James Jeans pinpointed the way of the future: *"The history of physical science in the twentieth century is one of progressive emancipation from the purely human angle of vision."* [5]

This was not, however, the aspect of science one cared to dwell upon. It was not sufficiently comforting. Earlier, Rutherford had shown that the atom is not solid but a tiny universe of energy whose nucleus and orbiting electrons are separated by vast space. Thus, if the actual mass of a human body were condensed, minus that energy-space, it would occupy an area about that of a pinhead. As Eiseley said, we are "process not reality." We are also illusion and, above all, energy. Eiseley concluded: "The fate of man is to be the ever recurrent, reproachful Eye floating upon night and solitude. The world cannot be said to exist save by the interposition of that inward eye—an eye various and not under the restraints to be apprehended from what is vulgarly called the natural." [6]

The theme echoes again and again, repeated by the members of the league of vision. That great naturalist Henry David Thoreau said, "Man cannot afford to be a naturalist, to look at nature directly, but only through the side of his eye. He must look through and beyond her." [7]

In an almost allegorical confrontation, a young poet of occult genius, Jean Cocteau, met the aged scientist Henri Poincaré. Of this meeting Cocteau wrote:

Where a wall forces philosophers and scholars to meticulous halts, the poet begins.

Science only serves to verify the discoveries of instinct.

I would like to quote two phrases to you. They were spoken to me by Henri Poincaré a few days before his death. . . . Here is the first sentence. "Why are you shy? It's for me to be shy. Your youth and poetry are two privileges. The chance of a rime sometimes makes a system emerge from darkness, and gaiety catches mystery on the wing."

The second was better. "Yes, yes," said this upright man, "I guess what it is. You would like to hear how far we have got with the unknown. Each day brings a miracle into our laboratories, but responsibility obliges us to maintain a professional silence. I see things, I see things . . ." (And he took off his eye-glasses.) "The confidence that is placed in us can only be maintained by certainty. The unknown!

"I heard the samovar and a passenger boat on the Seine.

"We hear it, at the present time, as miners excavating a tunnel hear the violent, muffled sounds and the first pickaxe blows of the miners on their way to meet them."

Admit it . . . not bad, was it? Moreover, it killed him. Outside forces made him die . . . the police force of the unknown.[8]

Yet he did *see* the power of the unknown. He saw its shadow, and partly its shape. One might almost say he *saw* its odor, for such a capacity does exist until the bars of a limited, professional "confidence" crash down with a dense, rationalist thud. In this sense, the artist is far freer than the scientist, but never less precise. Paul Klee said of the artist, "He neither serves nor rules—he transmits." [9]

And there are men of science who rank among the poets. In our time Theodor Schwenk, studying the movement of air and water, has arrived at an amazing synthesis of modern "objective" analysis and ancient intuitive understanding of the elements as spirit. He has also produced an astounding series of photographs to make visible a world of unseen, inner rhythm, at once natural and symbolic, a sigil of microcosm and macrocosm, a rare profile of the in-visible. These images reveal what happens when a stream of liquid flows into a body of still water. What emerges is a kaleidoscope of organic possibility, of architectural and symbolic richness. One sees a totem (Fig. 1), a fertilized ovule (Fig. 2), a mandala (Fig. 3), a phallus (Fig. 4). One sees a monolith strangely resembling the totemic heads of Easter Island, that speck of earth surrounded by a seeming infinity of water (Fig. 5). One sees a pelvic joint (Fig. 6), an avatar of bone and muscle "sculpted" as a momentary reflection of an eternal archetype—in water. One sees the budding of a floral form and the shadow of the atomic mushroom cloud. One sees the organic source of images that recur in the work of artists as seemingly disparate as J. M. W. Turner and Jean Arp.

Had a human being imagined and designed these forms, the Freudian interpretation would be generally predictable. But these images are not human. They are the work of a per-

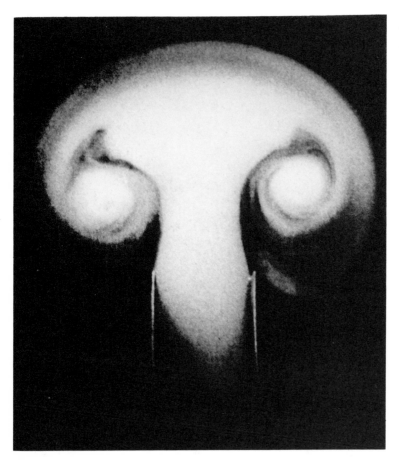

1–6. Various forms created by the flow of liquid into still water. Photos Verlag Freies Geistesleben, Stuttgart.

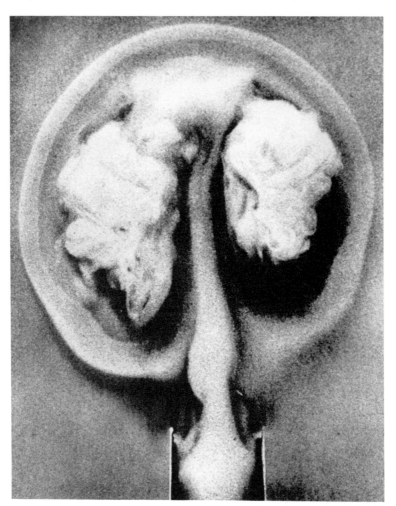

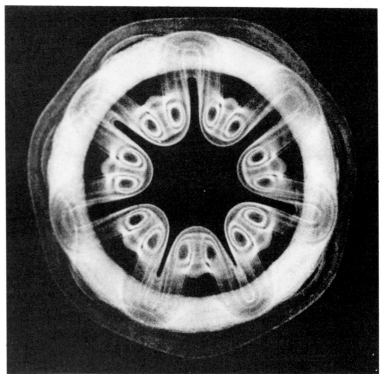

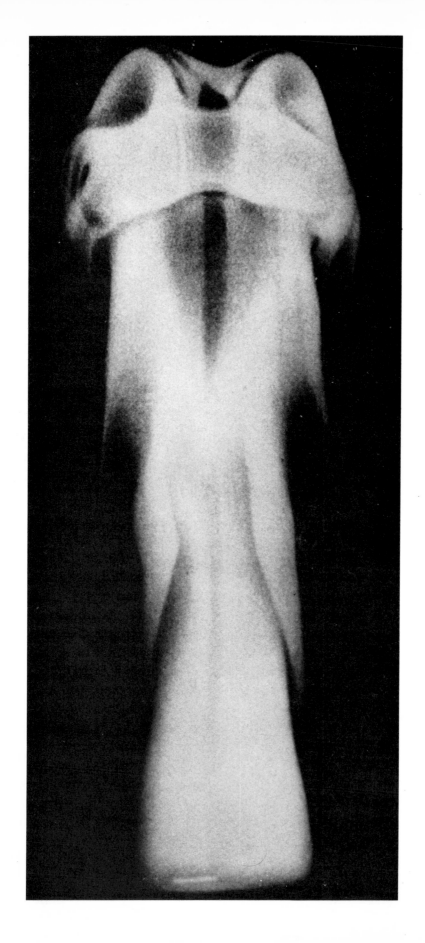

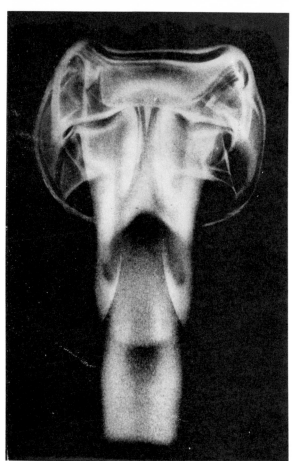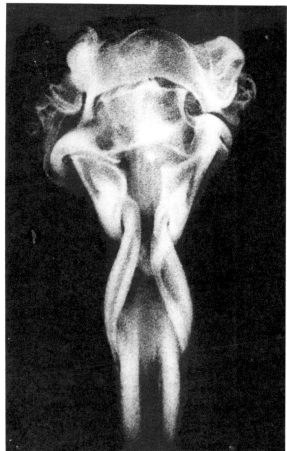

vasive spirit beyond the ego. They come out of a cosmic darkness, from the vast well of energy whose sources are unattainable by the mind. They rise, however, into the domain of what Jung called the collective unconscious. They hint at the meaning of what Thoreau saw and yearned for when he spoke of seeing "through and beyond" nature.

In his remarkable book, *Sensitive Chaos,* Schwenk makes the following observation:

Wherever water occurs it tends to take on a spherical form. It envelops the whole sphere of the earth, enclosing every object in a thin film. Falling as a drop, water oscillates about the form of a sphere; or as dew fallen on a clear and starry night it transforms an inconspicuous field into a starry heaven of sparkling drops.

We see moving water always seeking a lower level, following the pull of gravity. In the first instance it is earthly laws which cause it to flow, draw it away from its spherical form and make it follow a more or less linear and determined course. Yet water continually strives to return to its spherical form. It finds many ways of maintaining a rhythmical balance between the spherical form natural to it and the pull of earthly gravity. . . .

A sphere is a totality, a whole, and water will always attempt to form an organic whole by joining what is divided and uniting it in circulation. It is not possible to speak of the beginning or end of circulatory systems; everything is inwardly connected and reciprocally related. If a living circulation is interrupted, a totality is broken into and the linear chain of cause and effect as an inorganic law is set in motion.[10]

This should be perfectly acceptable, even to the confirmed rationalist, as a scientific proposition. However, the statement implies far more than that. It parallels to perfection the fundamental sense of occult knowledge. It reflects the endless circuit of the Tree of Life of the Holy Kabala, the meaning of the Wheel of Buddha and of the circular dance of Siva. Most of all, it finds its reflection in the Tarot or Taro, whose name knows two anagrams: Tora, Hebrew for *Law*; and Rota, which means the *Wheel*. The pack has been called, with appropriate symmetry, Tarota.

The nineteenth-century Mage Eliphas Lévi described the Tarot as embodying the whole wisdom of the Bible in a potent form that cuts beneath allegory or narrative. Indeed, the twenty-two major arcanas, keys or cards, express in symbolic language the entirety of human existence. Much scholarship has been devoted to exploring the origins of the pack; the only resulting conclusion is that, most appropriately, its origins are unknown. In itself it has no beginning and no end —like any perfect circle. The points along its perimeter are not 22 but infinite. When the deck is arranged as a circle, the Zero card, called the Fool (Fig. 7), reigns at the top, with arcana I (Fig. 8) to its right proceeding clockwise to arcana XXI (Fig. 9), on its left (see appendix).

Misdirected commentators take the Fool for a symbol of distraction, oblivion. On the contrary, he is the figure of a sublime and aloof consciousness beyond the human state, oblivious to the lynx, the crocodile, the precipice about him. He is a perfect equation of spirit. He is in the state of divine unity symbolized by *Oneness*.

Oswald Wirth, who was a disciple of Lévi's, remarked that

7. Tarot: Arc. O, *Le Mat* (The Fool). Woodcut, French, 1760.

8. Tarot: Arc. I, *Le Bateleur* (The Magician). Woodcut, French, 1760.

9. Tarot: Arc. XXI, *Le Monde* (The World, or The Universe). Woodcut, French, 1760.

"All comes from Nothing and returns to Nothing. But the *Nothing-Everything* is the Great Mystery, the Arcana of arcanas, before which reason confesses its impotence." [11] And a century later, Aleister Crowley taught that "The really important feature of this card is that its number should be 0. It represents therefore the Negative above the Tree of Life, the source of all things It is the Qabalistic Zero. It is the equation of the Universe, the initial and final balance of the opposites. . . ." [12]

Schwenk describes water (which is the element of all creation) as ever yearning for the wholeness of the sphere. He speaks of a rhythmical balance between that yearning and the pull of earthly gravity. As in nature, so in spirit, for the two are never apart. The Fool is that wholeness. He reigns between the Magician, wherein the creative urge begins, like a fertilized egg (again circular), complete but as yet unformed, and the World or Universe wherein the four elements are conjoined about a circle of consummation, the final apotheosis where, in T. S. Eliot's words: ". . . the tongues of fire are in-folded/Into the crowned knot of fire/ And the fire and the rose are one." [13] Yet this wholeness has been present throughout. Note that the Magician's hat takes the form of infinity: ∞.

The symbol-image truth of the great Zero is eternal. It is Siva, god of death and lord of the world, dancing at the center of the earth in a circle of flame, bearing the drum of creation and the flame of destruction in rhythmic, ever flowing equilibrium (Fig. 10). It is the divine circle in the brow of Buddha—the inner eye. In the Tibetan mandala it becomes a symbolic, concentric, infinite cosmology (Fig. 11), as it does in the Hebrew Holy Kabala, basis of the Tarot itself (Fig. 12). In Max Ernst's *Sun and Forest* (Fig. 13) paintings the sun becomes a magic circle, a perimeter—which puns the mechanical and the celestial, the natural and the symbolic. Late in Ernst's life, even the impenetrable forest was made to soften and dissolve, to become a magnetic field in the power of the solar-lunar circle (Fig. 14). In Giacometti's *The Chariot* (Fig. 15), the human flesh is pared away until it becomes a slender vibration, while the great wheels beneath become elements of power, reflections of cosmic move-

10. Siva as Lord of the Dance. Bronze, Madras State, Chola Dynasty, 11th C. Victoria & Albert Museum, London.

11. Painted Tanka with four Mandalas. Tibet, probably 15th C. Victoria & Albert Museum, London.

12. Cabalistic Diagram. Jewish, 16th C. Judeo-Contadin Synagogue Museum, France.

13. Max Ernst, *Sun and Forest*, 1926. Oil on canvas. Richard S. Zeisler Collection, N.Y.

14. Max Ernst, *The Last Forest*, 1960/69. Oil on canvas. Collection of the artist.

15. Alberto Giacometti, *The Chariot*. Bronze, 1950, 57″ x 26″ x 26⅛″. Collection, The Museum of Modern Art, N.Y.; Purchase.

ment; so might an archaic sculptor have depicted his gods borne through the heavens. A century earlier, Turner was drawn irresistibly, through nonsymbolic channels, into the vortex of the great Zero (Figs. 16–18). When Hazlitt quipped that Turner "paints nothing—and very like," [14] he was closer to the mark than he suspected. René Magritte painted the eye as its own mandala, its own sun, and its own universe (Fig. 19). For so it is. The retina is a mandala of perception, itself a microcosm. And there is wisdom in Magritte's title, *The False Mirror.* For the optic of "looking" is incomplete until it becomes the concentrated instrument of *seeing.* The symbol ∞ is also interpreted as the sign of the "third eye," wherein the sight of the two retinas becomes fused or alchemized into a luminous inner understanding. Thus, graphically as well as symbolically, $0 = \infty$.

At this point, however, a third mysterious card comes into play: arcana XV, Baphomet, or the Devil (Fig. 20). Here again is a key which only interpreters with creative insight have been able to discern. For the deep significance of arc. XV lies in the principle that if there were only Deity, and no force of opposition, there could exist only total perfection. Perfection, being complete Oneness, could never be divided into form; there could only be a celestial thought, a divine harmony, but not a world. The Devil, then, is the source of all worldly presences and desires. By definition, he is also the source of all excess, all disharmony, all evil. Wirth, conveying the teachings of Lévi, writes,

The serious adept does not forget that the Devil is the great magical agent, thanks to which miracles occur, unless they are of a purely spiritual order; for when mind acts directly upon mind, the Devil cannot intercede. But as soon as the body comes into play, nothing can be done without the Devil.[15]

Crowley comments:

This card represents creative energy in its most material form. . . . The card represents Pan Pangenetor, the All-Begetter. It is the Tree of Life as seen against a background of the exquisitely tenuous, complex, and fantastic forms of madness, the divine madness of spring, already foreseen in the meditative madness of winter.

16. J. M. W. Turner, *Snow Storm: Steam-Boat Off a Harbour's Mouth.* exh. 1842. Tate Gallery, London.

17. J. M. W. Turner, *Shade and Darkness—the Evening of the Deluge.* Oil on canvas, exh. 1843. Tate Gallery, London.

18. J. M. W. Turner, *Light and Colour (Goethe's Theory)—the Morning after the Deluge, Moses Writing the Book of Genesis.* Oil on canvas, exh. 1843. The Tate Gallery, London.

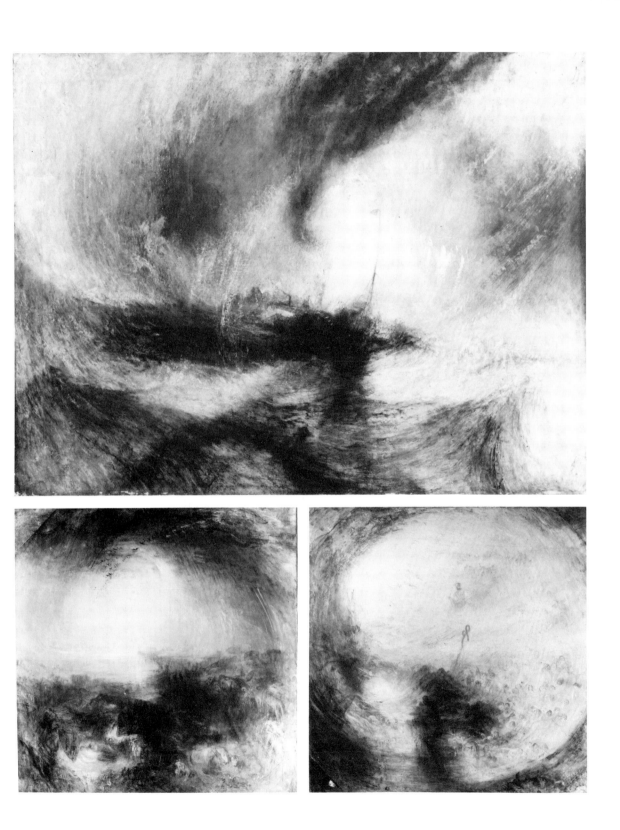

19. René Magritte, *The False Mirror*, 1928. Oil on canvas, 21¼″ x 31⅞″. Collection, The Museum of Modern Art, N.Y.; Purchase.

And he adds,

In every symbol of this card there is the allusion to the highest things and most remote. Even the horns of the goat are spiral, to represent the movement of the all-pervading energy. Zoroaster defines God as "having a spiral force." Compare the more recent, if less profound, writings of Einstein.[16] [Italics mine.]

Now between "the highest and most remote" and the lowest and most diabolical, there exists a logarithmic principle formulated without any deliberate reference to the occult by the medieval mathematician Leonardo Fibonacci da Pisa. The resulting "Fibonacci Curve" not only holds valid to our day but finds ever new applications as the perceptual means of science expand.

Fibonacci discovered that countless spirals in nature can be plotted according to a mathematical progression beginning with *one* and advancing by the addition of each *two* of the preceding numbers. Hence: 1, 1, 2, 3, 5, 8, 13, 21, 34, 55, 89, etc. This progression describes a constant scale of

20. Tarot: Arc. XV: *Le Diable* (The Devil). Woodcut, French, 1760.

21. Cross-section of nautilus shell. Galerie Michel Cachoux, Paris. Photo Clovis Prevost.

22. The Whirlpool Galaxy in Canes Venatici. Photographed with 200-inch telescope. Photo Hale Observatories, California Institute of Technology.

23. Hurricane viewed from the air. Photo Philips Corporation.

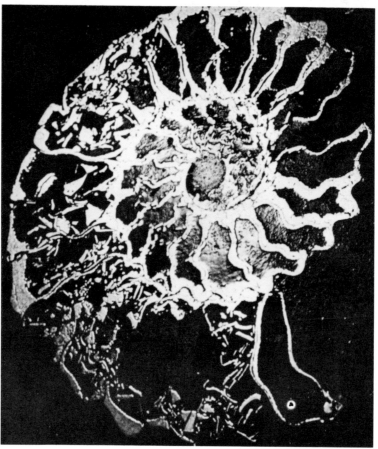

24. Fossil mollusk. Galerie Michel Cachoux, Paris. Photo Clovis Prevost.

ratios in the shape of spiral matter and suggests a fundamental rhythm in the spiral of creative energies. The law applies to the chambers of the nautilus shell (Fig. 21) as it does the curve of the Whirlpool Galaxy in the heavens (Fig. 22); it applies to the spin of a hurricane (Fig. 23) as to the rhythm of the mollusk's shell (Fig. 24); it applies to the curvature of a canary's claws as to the curve of the elephant's tusks, and equally to the spiral of the wild goat's horns. Crowley cites the helical motion in the Devil's goat horns, and uses not the science of Fibonacci but the mysticism of Zoroaster as his stated source. And he goes further: he equates, without even bothering to underline the point, the divine and diabolical spirals. He may or may not have known that Fibonacci had long since implicated nature. There is a great unity here, one we are bound to pursue.

In the fifteenth century, Butinone depicted the infant Christ upon a spiral throne, sigil of cosmic force, in his panel, *Christ Disputing with the Doctors* (Fig. 25). Either

25. Butinone, *Christ Disputing With the Doctors*, 15th C. Oil on panel. National Gallery of Scotland, Edinburgh. Annan Photographer, Glasgow.

time or faulty restoring have effaced part of a powerful companion symbol. Through the door of the chamber a tree in bloom rose from a still existing spiral of green earth. The two were meant as direct parallels, and as one: the helix of occult and spiritual Law and the helix of natural and creative Law.

Where that spiral begins and where it ends is an unanswerable question. It may indeed have no beginning and no end at all. *Ecclesiastes* 4:11 says: "He hath made every *thing* beautiful in His time: also He hath set the world in their heart, so that no man can find out the work that God maketh from the beginning to the end." The question remains a richly procreative mystery, an ever fluid equation that will never stand still. In our own time, D. H. Lawrence in England and Rémy de Gourmont in France chose to reformulate the story of Christ by suggesting that pagan illumination, the flesh, and the Moon Goddess were vital components lacking in the Christian schema. Julian the Apostate, Emperor of Rome, drew the same conclusion during the fourth century, and meant to restore pagan doctrines to official preeminence. One of the greatest "if's" in history is whether the whole of Western spiritual consciousness might not thus have taken a dramatic turn had Julian not died in battle at an early age.

In any case, the sinuous flow along which the high and the low become one, and in which the singular and the divided are linked, is the stream of creation. Inevitably the artist is drawn to this primal force: Jean Arp shaped it in marble and acutely described at least part of its mystery as an *Evocation of a Human, Lunar, Spectral Form* (Fig. 26). He had distilled in "modern" terms the creative-sexual-spiritual power which a fifth-century sculptor of Samothrace was able to identify in the precision of myth as *Aphrodite* (Fig. 27). It is the same rhythm, at heart, which animates the entwined fingers of Jean Ipousteguy's *The Lovers* (Fig. 28); again, the spiral, liquid—and fleshly—yearning for the perfect Zero is transfixed in marble.

In Arp's *Relief* (Fig. 29) the Zero is nearly consummated. In Hokusai's *Waterfall* (Fig. 30) the celestial Circle and its liquid torrents coincide inseparably. This eternal rhythm even turns up through what might be called willed chance on the

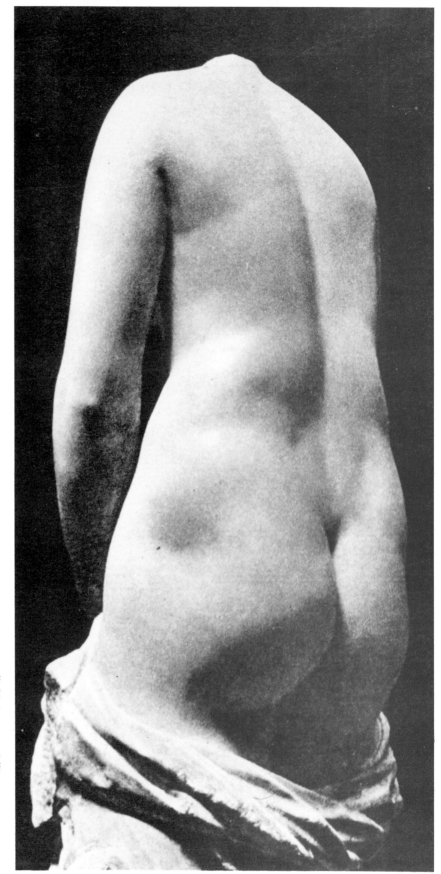

26. Jean Arp. *Evocation of a Human, Lunar, Spectral Form*, 1950. Marble. Collection Dotrement, Brussels.

27. *Aphrodite of Samothrace*. Greek, 5th C. Museum of Samothrace.

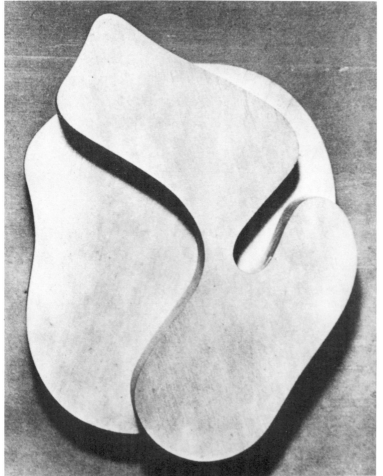

28. Jean Ipousteguy, *The Lovers* (detail), 1970. Marble. Galerie Claude Bernard, Paris.

29. Jean Arp, *Relief*, 1932. Bois de charme. Collection Michel Seuphor, Paris.

30. Hokusai, *The Waterfall*. Lithograph. Japanese, 19th C.

29

beautiful reverse of an Indian painting (Fig. 31). It is endless, and also inescapable. The Chinese poets who "signed" their "dreamstones" (Fig. 32) located the rhythm and the ultimate Zero ready-made in the stone of nature. For the spiral is in fact the great 0 and the great ∞ in their *active*, irrepressible, creative avatar in and out of time.

Yet, as suggested, the Devil too is a potent force here. Wirth writes, "The artist employs the Devil without binding himself to him by any pact." [17] That this is easier said than done is central to the artist's dilemma. The artist exists in an eternal state of paradox. He must delineate, separate, choose, limit, define, divide, in the attempt to join, unify,

31. Painting (Reverse of Lion Hunt), 1605. Indian, Mughal. Victoria & Albert Museum, London.

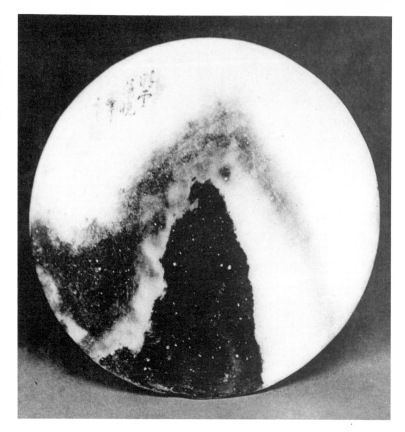

32. Dreamstone, Chinese, 19th C. *Bright Clouds Enveloping the Evening Peal.* Natural stone signed by Shih ch'uan. Photo Hugh Moss Ltd., London.

distill, purify towards the great wholeness, the sublime One. I = 0 is a godly equation; but the number of the Devil is two, the number of division, and the poet belongs to his world. Hence the poet is in the "devilish" position of having to alchemize the enigma, I = II, or, II = 0. He begins as arc. I in search of arc. XXI. He must circumnavigate the whole of the Great Wheel, forever in perilous suspension between the great Zero of the Fool and the Devil of free will and form.

The artist must deal with a concentric universe where to seek the heights means simultaneously to explore the depths. Biography speaks with eloquence of the perils involved. Dostoevsky aims at a complete spiritualization of man, yet falls into bitter excesses of temptation and creates havoc for all about him. Van Gogh achieves a rare and lucid sanity indecipherable to his contemporaries, is rejected, loses his precious balance, and spins into suicide. Paul Verlaine, having achieved the soulful heights of *Sagesses*, breaks down and is advised by a doctor to write out its darkling, carnal equivalent

—which he calls *Parallèlement*. DeQuincey climbs the ladder of imagination and finds himself mired in the miasmas of opium. Sade, Rimbaud, Bosch, Toulouse-Lautrec, Odilon Redon, Grünewald, Bresdin, Baudelaire, Huysmans, all learn to look directly into the black effulgence of Behemoth, for what is below is above, and what is above is below. Not so long after Crowley's death, Professor Crick and his associates at Cambridge discovered—in conformity with Zoroaster and Einstein—that the structure of the genetic principle is in fact a double helix, which they identified as D.N.A. And so it is that the deadly corkscrew-like syphilis bacillus, the genetic enemy that killed Manet, Baudelaire, Maupassant, and Gauguin, is helical as well.

. The duality, these dark roots of heaven, troubled Blake and became the mystery of his "Tyger, tyger, burning bright/ In the forests of the night." He had to ask: "What immortal hand or eye/Could frame thy fearful symmetry?" It was a terrible enigma, and he concluded with a question:

When the stars threw down their spears
And water'd heaven with their tears:
Did he smile his work to see?
Did he who made the Lamb make thee? [18]

Henri Rousseau vivified the same question (Fig. 33). Still, the tiger is part of an organic force. Only man is capable of upsetting that equilibrium. And this dire aspect is also

33. Henri Rousseau, *Tropical Storm, with a Tiger,* 1891 (detail). Oil on canvas. The National Gallery, London.

reflected perfectly in Schwenk's natural principle that "If a living circulation is interrupted, a totality is broken into," whereupon "an inorganic law is set in motion." This is precisely what has happened to our world of materialism, estranged from its underlying occult rhythms, out of touch with its wellsprings of archetypal knowledge—which is precisely what Blake warned about. We like to make a distinction between "hard thinking," which is sharp, concrete, solid, and "soft thinking," which is fuzzy, inexact, dull. So far as the rationalist level of induction and deduction goes, the distinction holds. But there is a third and more dynamic category of thought which can be called *fluid* thinking. This is a subtler zone of apprehending the nature of things, a more intuitive and more revelatory process. It implies an aptitude for sensing proportion and symbol, for receiving the vibrations of a universe of ubiquitous living presences, shapes, circulations, and sigils of mind and energy. It is the way of the poet and the magician, and it is increasingly the way of science.

One knows how, in the nineteenth century, the German chemist Kekulé discovered the molecular structure of benzine. All his best hard thinking had failed to produce a solution, but one night he had a dream. He dreamt of a serpent biting its own tail. On awakening, Kekulé *saw* the answer. It took the form of a closed carbon ring. Now carbon is the basic element of life, and the serpent biting its tail happens to be a very ancient symbol, the Ouroboros, at least as old as the Gnostic sects. J. E. Cirlot explains that "In the broadest sense, it is symbolic of time and of the continuity of life." [19] Here again is the great Zero, yet another circle and mandala, the image of the sphere which is also the true nature of water, the Nothing and Everything of the Tarot. And here it is again rediscovered, by a modern chemist, just as it was by the ancients, through intuitive and fluid processes; in fact, this time through the most fluid of all thought forms, the dream.

At the time, the event was doubtless taken down as a curiosity. Today, however, the situation has changed vastly, because science increasingly finds itself enmeshed in a cosmic tapestry of the impossible. The subatomic physicist must incessantly account for what he cannot intellectually believe:

an electron changes from one orbit to another without ever having traveled through space; an electron fired at a screen with two holes in it goes through both apertures at once; a positron, or double-negative electron, can only be explained as moving backwards in time; a neutrino, which has no mass, no charge, and no magnetic field—and which hence cannot truly be said to exist—passes through our bodies and through the crust of the earth as if those "objects" did not exist for it—in fact, quite like a ghost.

In an attempt to begin to explain the unexplainable, physicists have been compelled to speak of what they term the *psi field*. The term implies a dimension or zone of reality along which events occur beyond the plane of cause and effect explicable in our "normal" world. In other words: such and such has been seen to happen; but it cannot have happened within our range of causal understanding; therefore there must be an angle of reality-vision, a dimension, to encompass the phenomenon. The term is vague, of course—but it is intrinsically more scientific than the easier pretension that any given evidence must be invalid because it fails to accommodate the theory.

Heraclitus wrote, "If you do not expect it, you will not find the unexpected, for it is hard to find and difficult." [20] Many centuries later Louis Pasteur laid down the law that "In the field of observation, chance favors the mind prepared." [21] We are involved here with the art of skepticism and the art of belief. One might postulate another law: Skepticism can only be said to exist where the capacity for belief exists. In other words, to say, "I'm a skeptic, I don't believe that sort of thing," is not skepticism at all. Skepticism begins: "I can't believe this; I shall have to explore it thoroughly."

Thus, the "psi field" is the postulation of faith in scientific method. It consists of what Arthur Koestler calls "a verbal raft," a framework for further investigating the evidence. Strangely, however, parapsychologists had spoken of a psi field long before the subatomic physicists. The latter came to it reluctantly, rationally, ineluctably. The former came to it instinctively, gladly, through the path of acknowledgment. They were less concerned with the fact that extrasensory perception, a clairvoyant capacity to predict the future, the luminous cropping up of the invisible, the elegant if eerie symmetry of coincidence, could not be "proven" systematically. The fact of love cannot be explained, and the luminosity of art cannot be systematized either. The fact of their existence imposes itself upon the receptive mind; where there is no receptivity, they in effect cease to exist. Behind La Rochefoucauld's little gem of cynicism, "There are people who would never have loved had they never heard of love," [22] lies the truth that the belief fathers the capacity. Only at that point does skepticism cease to be obstructive and become essential.

For the ancients, this psi field never had to be postulated because it was too evident, too obvious. The goddess was a fact; it sufficed to consult the moon, to acknowledge the sun, to witness the stones. These were living things, not objects. Not every ancient knew how to read the signs of "natural" objects, but he had his seers. And the seer was not a creator, in our sense, but a man of knowledge in a sense now largely lost. The earth was not matter but energy, and flesh was a far more living energy, the vibrating coffer of secrets, a receptor, a transmitter. The mind-body was a computer, not of quantitative sums but of qualitative equations. In the end the ancients too denied their seers, so that the secrets had to be passed from hand to hand, from cult to cult.

Throughout time, certain artists have devoted themselves to worship of the psi field. No matter that they had never heard the term expressed; they saw it embodied as a rhythm. They saw the shape and body and vibration of a rhythmic light. Modern art has evolved the convenient term "abstraction." But abstraction is beside the point. The poet-magician knows no abstractions, only powers and realities.

Carlos Castaneda has published what he terms the chronicles of his experience with the Yaqui Indian seer called Don Juan. This account whether of actual experience or, as some have suggested, of entirely hallucinogenic inspiration, is a text of great significance. It is a magician's log of power over what Schwenk called sensitive chaos and what the Tarot represents as an ubiquity of spirit in the affairs of men.

Don Juan awakens Castaneda to the immanent life of all

things, to the spirits of the earth and desert. He takes this naive and sincere anthropologist into the wilderness and shows that every solitude and pinnacle and distance is tremulous with spirit. He proves that dimension is endless, that direction is as important as place, that *here* is no more real than the vector of south-east or north-west, that the pervasive spirit can exalt or kill depending upon the will and equilibrium of the seeker, that the earth contains a viscera of spirit and every particle of space a medium of mind. He proves the invisible. He demonstrates that there is no inner and outer, but only a consciousness that permeates rock and flesh and space. He shows that matter and mind are but manifestations of the same *field*.

Don Juan tells his pupil: "What a sorcerer calls will is a power within ourselves. It is not a thought, or an object, or a wish. . . . Will is what can make you succeed when your thoughts tell you that you're defeated. Will makes you invulnerable. Will is what sends a sorcerer through a wall; through space; to the moon, if he wants." And he went on to say: "Will is a force, a power. *Seeing* is not a force, but rather a way of getting through things. A sorcerer may have a very strong will and yet he may not *see*; which means that only a man of knowledge perceives the world with his senses and with his will and also with his *seeing*." [23]

What Don Juan means by seeing is, at heart, a vision of the inner structures of life, their internal forms and rhythms, their archetypal images, their pulses and vibrations—until the gods and demiurges become visible. All this cannot be evoked by logic or by reason, by processes of induction or deduction. It can only be illuminated by that psychic-perceptive working of the inner eye, that carnal-ascetic working of the hand, through which magic becomes manifest.

For science, the psi field is an idea, inexpressible by any image. The Greek letter *psi* was chosen for its very neutrality. In parallel, Don Juan told Castaneda to try to "hear" reality rather than to look at it, for he knew that the mental-optical process is corrupted by appearances and associations. One remembers that the Old Testament forbade the making of graven images as a sacrilege before Spirit. Yet certain artists have managed to conjure up pure screens of rhythm, images of vibration that are not really images at all, and which might be called portraits of the psi dimension.

Like Turner, Victor Hugo touched what the Eastern seers called the Tao, now alias Psi. Using films or screens of lace he invented the first *collages* and first *frottages* in modern painting; using thumb prints he became the first western *tachiste*. Using inks and folded paper (Fig. 34), he produced those mysterious and semisymmetrical forms which would only interest the world when reinvented a century later by the psychologist Rorschak. Hugo inscribed his initials in celestial compositions of psi power (Fig. 35) and depicted his own destiny as a primal surge of the wave (Fig. 36). He juggled the ego and the cosmos with a leonine grace and a similar arrogance. Jean Cocteau could later say, "Victor Hugo was a madman who thought he was Victor Hugo." [24] To see his

34. Victor Hugo, *Ink Spot, Intimation of a Bridge*, c. 1850. Ink, wash, and folded paper. Collection Jean Hugo. Photo Bulloz, Paris.

35. Victor Hugo, *Initials*, c. 1860. Maison Victor Hugo, Paris. Photo Bulloz, Paris.

36. Victor Hugo, *The Wave* (or, *My Destiny*), 1857. Ink, wash, and gouache. Maison Victor Hugo, Paris. Photo Bulloz, Paris.

nineteenth-century illuminations as a precocious forerunner of "abstract" art would be at least partially error, for Tao or Psi flow through time just as neutrinos pass through matter. As we shall see, time and light are the media of the great Unity. In this respect it is a distortion to see the psi facades of a Paul Klee, a Mark Tobey, a Manfred Schwartz or an Henri Michaux simply as examples of contemporary abstraction. Klee sought out the numinous in terms of vibrations; hence, the energy screens of *Walpurgisnacht* (Fig. 37) and of *Garden of the Chateau* (Fig. 38). Tobey lived in the East, absorbed the sentient rhythms of Oriental calligraphy, and transmuted their sense into passages of resounding light (Fig. 39). Schwartz saw the creative fluid transmogrified in the glistening pebbles of a beach at Etretat, and alchemized what he saw into a timeless frieze of light beyond color (Fig. 40). Tobey worked from East to West, Schwartz from West

37. Paul Klee, *Walpurgis-nacht*, 1935. Gouache. Tate Gallery, London.

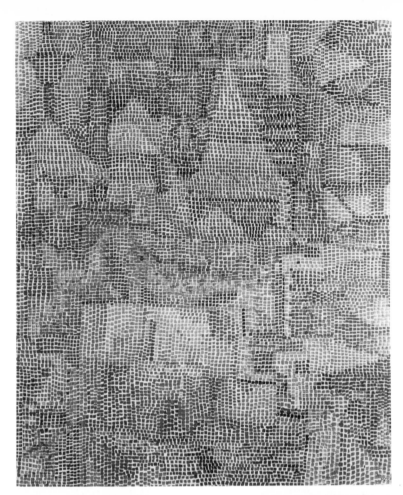

38. Paul Klee, *Garden of the Chateau*, 1935. Gouache. Private collection. Photo Bulloz, Paris.

39. Mark Tobey, *Crossed Lives*, 1965. Tempera. Private collection. Photo Luc Jobert, courtesy Galerie Jeanne Bucher, Paris.

40. Manfred Schwartz, *Etretat: Falaise d'Aval*, 1960. Charcoal. Private collection. Photo Knoedler & Co., N.Y.

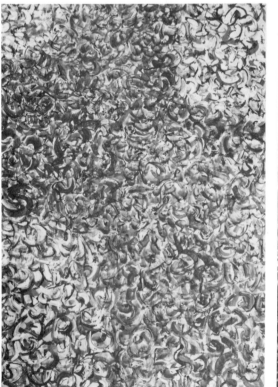

41. Henri Michaux, *Untitled*, 1961. Chinese ink on paper. Le Point Cardinal, Paris. Photo Jacqueline Hyde.

42. Joseph Sima, *Untitled*, 1967. Oil on canvas. Private collection, Paris. Le Point Cardinal, Paris. Photo Jacqueline Hyde.

to East. Michaux found his vibrations through the aegis of hallucinatory drugs (Fig. 41), and Joseph Sima through a meditative sobriety. And in more than one work (Fig. 42), Sima chose to conceal an egg—occult symbol of generation and life—within the limitless psi swarm.

In the same way, the primal power of light took Georges Seurat beyond the formal confines of pointillism just as it took Hugo beyond the bounds of Romanticism. Seurat's

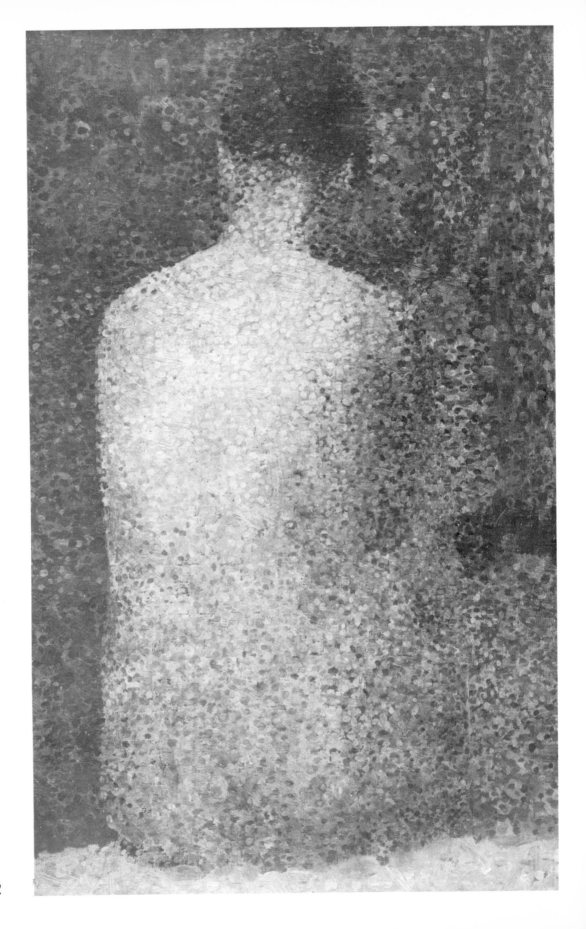

42

43. Georges Seurat, *Seated Nude*, 1887. Oil on canvas. Jeu de Paume, Musée du Louvre, Paris. Photo Bulloz.

44. Victor Hugo, *The Chateau of Cries-in-the-Night*, c. 1860. Wash. Maison Victor Hugo. Photo Bulloz, Paris.

Seated Nude (Fig. 43) and Hugo's *Chateau of Cries-in-the-Night* (Fig. 44) are each in their different ways architectures of the possibilities of light. Meanwhile, science has conjured its own magic in the form of a laser beam: light honed to a power capable of sundering steel or of healing a retina. Of such extremes of strength and delicacy are art and magic woven.

The Non-self

The will to purity, toward a celebration of pure light, also implies a response to Baphomet, to terrestrial divisions— and to the ego. The poet and magician martial the self in order to transcend the self. This is the way of lucid mysticism. Now, for the first time in many centuries, the mystical way falls within the purview of science. The words written by Alfred North Whitehead in 1938 ratify the vision of Blake:

Matter has been identified with energy, and energy is sheer activity. The modern point of view is expressed in terms of energy, activity and the vibratory differentiations of space-time. Any local agitation shakes the whole universe. The distant effects are minute, but they are there. The concept of matter presupposed simple location . . . but in the modern concept the group of agitations which we term matter is fused into its environment. *There is no possibility of a detached, self-contained existence.*[25] [Italics mine.]

The members of the league of vision have expatiated this point in many ways. For Aldous Huxley, the drug mescalin opened the gates of matter upon the miracles of energy. He describes the transfiguration of a bouquet of three bright flowers: "At breakfast that morning I had been struck by the lively dissonance of its colours. But that was no longer the point. I was not looking now at an unusual flower arrangement. I was seeing what Adam had seen on the morning of his creation—the miracle, moment by moment, of naked existence." He spoke of it as ". . . a transcience that was yet eternal life, a perpetual perishing that was at the same time pure Being, a bundle of minute, unique particulars in which, by some unspeakable and yet self-evident paradox, was to be seen the divine source of all existence." Under the influence of the drug each and every object bespoke a "sacramental vision of reality": "The legs, for example, of that chair—how miraculous their tubularity, how supernatural their polished smoothness! I spent several minutes—or was it several centuries?—not merely gazing at those bamboo legs, but actually *being* them—or rather being myself in them; or, to be still more accurate (for 'I' was not involved in the case, nor in a certain sense were 'they') being my Not-self in the Not-self which was the chair." [26]

Sacrament, non-self, cosmic connection, the vision of oneness revealed—these form the invisible trapeze of the acrobat-seer poised between the Fool and Baphomet. Paul Klee, as if struck by a dazzling light, cried out:

Am I God? I have accumulated so many great things in me! My head aches to the point of bursting. It has to hold an overflow of power. May you want (are you worthy of it?) that it be born in you. (Aside:) They also were not worthy of Him they crucified.

More realistically: Genius sits in a glass house—but in an unbreakable one—conceiving ideas. After giving birth, it falls into madness. Stretches out its hand through the window toward the first person happening by. The demon's claw rips, the iron fist grips. Before you were a model, mocks the iron voice between serrated teeth, for me, you are raw material to work on. I throw you against the glass wall, so that you remain stuck there, projected and stuck. . . . (Then come the lovers of art and contemplate the work from outside. . . .) [27]

This was the madness the surrealists pursued through dreams in search of a luminous "paranoia." Ernst tracked it down with a magical cunning. Klee dived for it through the dream-depths of childhood. When the mind is altered, jogged off course, unsettled, it begins to respond to new lights and new vibrations. The irritation of sensitive membranes is what causes the oyster to generate its pearl. No one has spoken of this theme more brilliantly than Herman Melville in *Moby Dick*, when he described how Pip, the cabin boy, was recovered from the sea alive but witless:

The sea had jeeringly kept his finite body up, but drowned the infinite of his soul. Not drowned entirely, though. Rather carried down alive to wondrous depths, where strange shapes of the unwarped primal world glided to and fro before his passive eyes; and the miser-merman, Wisdom, revealed his hoarded heeps; and among the joyous, heartless, ever juvenile eternities, Pip saw the multitudinous, God-omnipresent, coral insects, that out of the firmament of waters heaved the colossal orbs. He saw God's foot upon the treadle of the loom, and spoke of it; and therefore his shipmates called him mad. So man's insanity is heaven's sense; and wandering from all mortal reason, man comes at last to that celestial thought, which, to reason, is absurd and frantic; and weal or woe, feels them uncompromised, indifferent as his God.[28]

Thus, by elevation or catastrophe, by privileged sobriety or by intoxication, by chance or by will, the self and spirit are capable of moving apart, of meshing together, and often of regarding each other in a moment of ecstasy or horror. The medium goes into a light or heavy trance and ceases to be in one sense while magnifying his being in another.

In *The Babylon Lottery*, the Argentine writer Jorge Luis Borges touches the theme of non-self with particular sensitivity to the psi corridors of the magician himself:

Like all men in Babylon I have been a proconsul; like all, a slave. Look again: through this rent in my cape you can see a ruddy tattoo on my belly. It is the second symbol, Beth. This letter, on nights of full moon, gives me power over men whose mark is ghimel. In a cellar at dawn I have severed the jugular of sacred bulls against a black rock. During one lunar year I have been declared invisible; I shrieked and was not heard, I stole my bread and was not decapitated. I have known what the Greeks did not: uncertainty. In a bronze chamber, faced with the silent handkerchief of the strangler, hope has been faithful to me; in the river of delights, panic has not failed me.[29]

This passage was born of a cold though fluid intellectual sobriety. It becomes interesting to compare it with another, written one century and a half earlier by Thomas de Quincey. Autobiographical, it describes a vision induced by opium:

I was stared at, hooted at, grinned at, chattered at, by monkeys, by peroquets, by cockatoos. I ran into pagodas: and was fixed, for centuries, at the summit, or in secret rooms; I was the idol; I was the priest; I was worshipped; I was sacrificed. I fled from the wrath of Brama through all the forests of Asia: Vishnu hated me: Seeva laid wait for me. I came suddenly upon Isis and Osiris: I had done a deed, they said, which the ibis and the crocodile trembled at. I was buried, for a thousand years, in stone coffins, with mummies and sphynxes, in narrow chambers at the heart of eternal pyramids. I was kissed with cancerous kisses by crocodiles; and laid, confounded with all unutterable slimy things, amongst reeds and Nilotic mud.[30]

As in Huxley's experience the element of time is unhinged and obliterated. And as in the case of both Huxley and Borges the self shifts, slides, is eclipsed, and is recreated in the field of another and mysterious power. The "I" somehow abides and endures, yet so variously as not to be a first person singular at all; it is its self and not its self. It remains aware of its "self," but as a seeming whole that is really only a part.

All three testaments, hallucinatory or not, are the products of greatly cultivated minds, all sophisticated and all prone to aesthetics. Such, however, was not the case of a preadolescent girl who presented her father one Christmas with a manuscript relating a sequence of her dreams. The father, appropriately alarmed, brought the collection to Carl G. Jung who pronounced them the weirdest he had ever seen. Among the "relevant motifs" transcribed by Jung in his own words are the following:

"The evil animal," a snakelike monster with many horns, kills and devours all other animals. But God comes from the four corners, being in fact four separate gods, and gives rebirth to all the dead animals.

An ascent into heaven, where pagan dances are being celebrated; and a descent into hell, where angels are doing good deeds.

A small mouse is penetrated by worms, snakes, fishes and human beings. Thus the mouse becomes human. This portrays the four stages of the origins of mankind.

There is a desert on the moon where the dreamer sinks so deeply into the ground that she reaches hell.

The girl becomes dangerously ill. Suddenly birds come out of her skin and cover her completely.[31]

Of the twelve dreams in all, Jung identified nine as "influenced by the theme of destruction and restoration," and as more closely oriented to "primitive" myth than to Christian formulations at that time. Even where Christian concepts apply—as in the idea of *Apokatastasis* or restitution—the ten-year-old girl could have had no contact with them.

As to the first dream, with God coming from the four corners, Jung had to ask the question: The four corners of what? No enclosure or room is specified, and none would fit in with so cosmic a panorama. On the other hand, the concept of the quaternity is a medieval representation which disappeared in favor of the trinity, save in the most esoteric scholarship, during the eighteenth century. Jung, who was a prodigious scholar of alchemical doctrine, felt he was able to identify a four-horned serpent (*quadricornicus serpens*) as an "antagonist of the Christian Trinity." Any knowledge of such esoterica on the child's part was quite out of the question.

The second dream, apart from Jung's thesis, broaches a theme far beyond the understanding of any child: the great duality of above and below, of heaven and hell, of the very mingling of Deity and Behemoth which we have touched upon. Here is the sense of the violent passion of Arthur Rimbaud—whom François Mauriac called *"le crucifié malgré lui"*—of Bosch's ambiguous *Garden of Earthly Delights*, of Georges Rouault's saints and harlots, of Picasso's satyrs and fawns, courtesans and nuns.

As Jung stated, the third dream recapitulates human evolution in a manner quite beyond the girl's capacities. And the fourth and fifth dreams present surrealist imagery in eerie fashion: the moon-desert-hell dream suggests in varying ways the metaphors of Joan Miró or Yves Tanguy; the bird dream recalls the images of Salvador Dali or, again, Max Ernst.

The ensemble troubled Jung greatly. These dreams were appropriate not to a young person approaching puberty, with a new life ahead, but to an older human being laden with thought, preparing for departure. Just over one year later the girl contracted an infectious disease and died.

Several points should be stressed. This is not an instance of a single recurrent symbolic dream. It amounts to a bewildering symbolist anthology on the part of an unlikely source. Furthermore, however somber they may seem to the reader these dreams were not seen by the child as morbid or daunting. Instead, she offered them as a present, as part of her reality. She had no history of mental trouble, and no chronic illness.

How then can the enigma be explained? The experience, cutting across plausible lines of time and causality, raises the mystery of the psi field. This is a case of extrasensory knowledge or perception transmitted in the dream state, and a case of prophecy as well. The dreams themselves offer a number of clues; they begin to suggest in their imagery a kind of psychic map of the territory in which the poet-magician navigates his goetic course. I shall try to develop a picture of that world in terms of a strange, simultaneous double image: the labyrinth and the desert.

The Labyrinth and the Desert

The first dream is perhaps the oddest of all, given its blend of physical and nonphysical elements, of place and nonplace, of matter and energy. The image is truly kaleidoscopic. The one God becomes four; the dead are restored to life; the "corners" belong to no discernible plane of space. There is a dynamic flux of life-energy in which the only situation of space at all is the presence of four cardinal points.

J. E. Cirlot gives us a crucial definition of the fact-idea represented by the word *precinct*:

Precinct. All images to do with the precinct—an enclosure, a walled garden, a city, a square, a castle, a *patio*—correspond to the idea of the *temenos*, or a sacred and circumscribed place which is guarded and defended because it constitutes a spiritual entity. Such images as this may also symbolize the life of the individual and in particular the inner life of his thoughts. It will be recognized that a square or circle is the tactical formation commonly adopted as a means of defence in a critical situation against a more powerful adversary. This in itself would suffice to explain the meaning of the mandala, or any of the innumerable symbols that are based upon the notion of the precinct or the protection of a given space, identified with the self.[32]

Butinone's *Christ Disputing with the Doctors* is rich in this sense, as are so many works of the Renaissance. The chamber becomes more than a room, the building more than an edifice; these become vessels of spiritual force and containment, and truly magical precincts. Sassetta expresses this element in his panels of the life of St. Francis (Fig. 45). This deeply harmonious instinct is maximized by Giotto, and by Duccio before him at the very juncture of medieval and Renaissance consciousness.

The vision is timeless—and endlessly various. Georges Noel balances a labyrinth of *directions* as open as those of the little girl's dream (Fig. 46). In Magritte's *The Reckless Sleeper* (Fig. 47) the very fluidity of the dream freezes into labyrinthine fixity. The Aztecs (Fig. 48) meticulously enclose a temple within a precinct of protection; whereas Turner explodes the gracious confines of Petworth to admit a whirlwind of creative light (Fig. 49). Giorgio de Chirico dwarfs the modern precinct before a limitless desert of mythological possibility (Fig. 50); and Magritte instead boxes precinct within precinct, sigil of the modern dilemma (Fig. 51).

Picasso places the hell of *Guernica* (Fig. 52) in an open plaza that mysteriously becomes a closed, lamp-lit chamber. In *The Family* (Fig. 53) Miró inscribes a wriggling nebula of biological presences within a room whose one window is sainted by the cosmic eye.

And the eye forms a crucial connection: Plotinus said that the eye could not see the sun were it not a kind of sun itself; and the Egyptians, as Cirlot testifies, defined the eye as

45. Sassetta, *The Whim of S. Francis to Become a Soldier* (1430–32). Panel from an altarpiece. The National Gallery, London.

46. Georges Noel, *Untitled*, 1972. Sand, polymer, binder ink and graphite on canvas. Pace Gallery, N.Y. Photo Al Mozell.

47. René Magritte, *The Reckless Sleeper*, 1927. Oil on canvas. Tate Gallery, London.

48. Plan of an Aztec temple, no date given. British Museum.

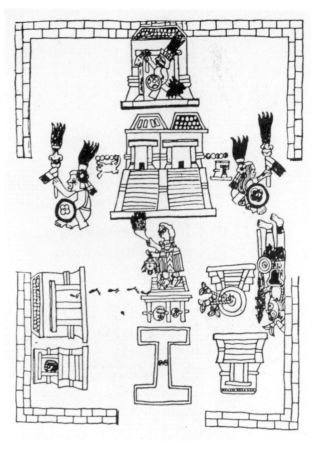

49. J. M. W. Turner, *Interior at Petworth*, c. 1837. Oil on canvas. Tate Gallery, London.

50. Giorgio de Chirico, *Roman Villa*, 1922. Private collection. Oil on canvas. Photo Giraudon, Paris.

51. René Magritte, *In Praise of Dialectics*, 1937. Oil on canvas. National Gallery of Victoria, Melbourne, Felton Bequest, 1971.

52. Pablo Picasso, *Guernica*, 1937 (May–early June). Oil on canvas, 11' 5½" x 25' 5¾". On extended loan to The Museum of Modern Art, N.Y., from the artist.

53. Joan Miró, *The Family*, 1924. Black and red chalk on emery paper, 29½" x 41". Collection, The Museum of Modern Art, N.Y. Gift of Mr. and Mrs. Jan Mitchell.

the "sun in the mouth," or the creative Word. Thus the eye is itself a mandala, precinct and microcosm, as well as a Great Zero, a solar-lunar force. Odilon Redon represents it as such, most mystically—a flowering orb that outshines its rectangular (mortal) precinct (Fig. 54). Unintentionally, the same verity was diagrammed centuries earlier in an anatomical painting that shows the eye to be a blazing sphere within its temporary precinct of muscle and bone (Fig. 55).

Max Ernst's *At the First Clear Word* (Fig. 56) defines the precinct in particularly heraldic language. Here the wall-precinct becomes a zone of contention in the field of occult power. On either side, nature blooms with intrepid grace, while the human hand fails to carry out its organic mission. The red bulb or plunger puns the ripe berries, but its connection with the insect is absurd, flaccid, powerless. And the hand itself is significant. The thumb, second only to the brain, is the one vital structure that separates men from apes. Indian chiromancers once told fortunes from the thumb alone, and Chinese sages merely from the thumb's first phalanx. But here this symbol of man hangs limp, useless. The bulb is held impossibly between the middle finger, which chiromancy places under the sign of Saturn, and the index finger, ascribed to Jupiter. The saturnine heaviness crosses out and annuls the Jupiterian will. The fourth fin-

54. Odilon Redon, *L'oeil au Pavot*, c. 1880–85. Charcoal. Private collection. Photo Bulloz.

55. J. F. Gautier-d'Agoty, *Etching*, 1706. Galerie J. C. Gaubert, Paris. Photo Heidi Meister.

ger (Apollo) is known as the center of personal affection—which explains why it became the "ring finger" on which a wedding band is classically worn; and the little finger (Mercury) is the point of instinct and of sexuality. Both of these are here indrawn, invisible. The wall, as precinct, like the walls of *Guernica*, now assumes a negative and deadly charge. In surreal parallel, Pierre Roy's *Danger On the Stairs* (Fig. 57) admits that deady helix, the serpent, within the confines of a modern, protective precinct. The charmed circle is broken; the demon enters.

In the case of the young girl's dream the precinct is not closed and protective, but merely incipient and open to onslaughts of power. It is a barely situated field of activity. Don Juan's desert is full of such ambiguity and danger in its alive vastness. And central to Cirlot's definition is the fact that the *precinct* is at once physical and psychological, tangible and symbolic. As symbol of the individual's inner life it becomes a labyrinth woven of the limitless mind-desert in which it is erected.

That nexus is ideally reflected in the Hindu god Vishnu.

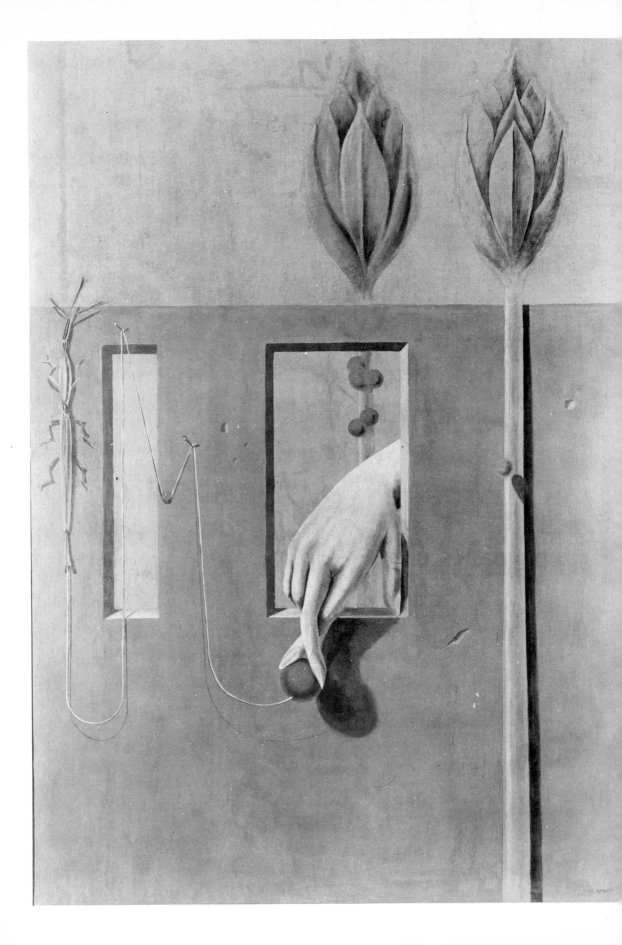

56. Max Ernst, *At the First Clear Word*, 1923. Oil on panel. Galerie André François Petit, Paris. Photo Giraudon.

57. Pierre Roy, *Danger on the Stairs*, 1927 or 1928. Oil on canvas, 36″ x 23⅝″. Collection, The Museum of Modern Art, N.Y. Gift of Abby Aldrich Rockefeller.

In the early Vedic texts, he was conceived of in terms of light alone, light penetrating the entirety of the universe. Later he assumed 10, then 22, then endless avatars of anthropomorphic form. In the nineteenth century, an Indian painter portrayed him (Fig. 58) asleep upon the serpent of eternity, in the cosmic waters, beside his wife Lakshmi, symbol of love

The Labyrinth and the Desert 57

and beauty. From his sleep—the sleep of creative cycles—the cosmic man is born out of a flower Blake would have recognized. The image is fluid, generative, again a circular motion tending to our most perfect of precincts, the Great Zero.

58. *Vishnu on the Serpent of Eternity*. Indian miniature, Kangra, 19th C. Victoria & Albert Museum, London.

A century later, Tàpies deals with a pair of spectacles—the optic as object—to draw this spherically oriented motion into a very fixed precinct wherein energy is held, confined, in stasis (Fig. 59). The poet and painter incessantly fluctuate between these two poles of fluidity—which makes creation possible—and fixity, which makes expression possible. In this connection, the strange and tragic case of Antonin Artaud becomes a *cause célèbre*.

Artaud was not led to destruction, he was born to it. The dissolution of the self and the act of suicide were there from the beginning. One imagines a mythological monstrosity, half cripple, half strongman, a fated plaything of magic rather than its perceptor.

Born in Marseille in 1896, Artaud arrived in Paris at twenty-four, a unique if undisciplined poet. Jacques Rivière, editor of the *Nouvelle Revue Française,* refused to publish his poems but, intrigued, asked to meet the man who wrote them. A correspondence ensued, and Artaud explained:

I suffer from a frightful disease of the mind. My thought abandons me at all stages. From the simple act of thinking to the external act of its materialization in words. Words, forms of phrases, inner directions of thinking, simple reactions of the mind —I am in constant pursuit of my intellectual being. . . . I am beneath myself, I know it, it makes me suffer, but I accept the fact in the fear of not dying entirely. . . .

I have felt and accepted these ungainly expressions which you criticize. Bear in mind: I have not questioned them. They come from the deep uncertainty of my thinking. Fortunate indeed when this uncertainty is not replaced by the absolute inexistence from which I sometimes suffer.[33]

And he wrote that "Those who've attributed more life to me . . . are lost in the darkness of man." But Artaud was either short of that attribute or somewhere beyond it. He was a field of energy, a zone acted upon.

59. Anton Tàpies-Puig, *The Spectacles,* 1966. Oil and composition. Galerie Claude Bernard, Paris.

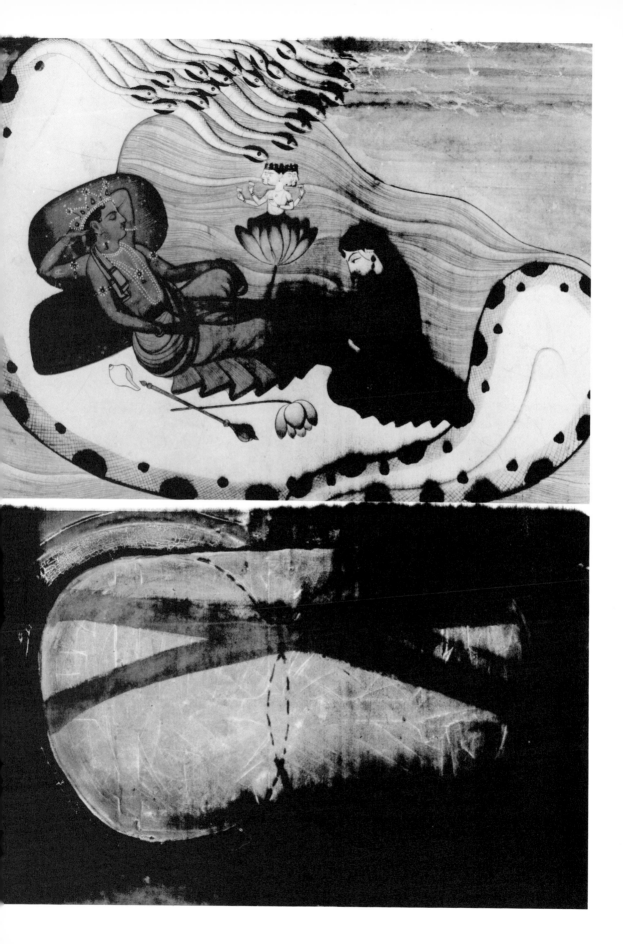

The difficulty really is in finding one's place and rediscovering communication with one's self. Everything lies in a certain flocculation of things, in an assortment of all these mental stones around a point which is precisely what we are searching for.

And here is what I, Artaud, think of thought: INSPIRATION DOES EXIST;

And there is a phosphorescent point where all reality is rediscovered, but changed, metamorphosed—and by what?—a point open for the *magic* use of things. And I believe in mental meteors, in individual cosmogonies.

Do you know what suspended sensitivity is, this frightening vitality schismed in two. This point of necessary cohesion where being no longer rises. This menacing, this overwhelming place.[34]

It was in pursuit of that "point open for the *magic* of things" that Artaud began to give eerily shaped form to his wavering existence. His knowledge of the occult keys—the Kabala, the Tarot, astrology and numerology, in their most sober aspect—deepened by instinct as by tenacity. He went into the desert, to Mexico, where an abundant magic came to hand, abetted by the drug peyote, ancient threshold of hallucinatory access, cousin to Huxley's mescalin and Don Juan's "little smoke." Drugs would also be the medium of his doom. But Artaud saw this from the beginning, and lived with it, while he moved outward—and inward—under incredible pressure. In the deathly landscape of the Mexican desert he found new specters of reality:

. . . It is the act which shapes our thought. As for matter and mind, the Mexicans know only the concrete. And the concrete never tires of functioning, of drawing something from nothing: this is the secret we want to go and ask of the descendants of high Mexican civilizations.[35]

What Artaud found was that the voice had penetrated the land. He found in the sea of twisted totemic rock the "strange signatures" of the gods, in images, recurrent signs, where "a whole country develops on stone a philosophy parallel to that of men." Then he went still further, and found an austere vocabulary of numbers, which he saw repeated again and again in stone as an arcane leitmotif:

There is in the Kabala a music of Numbers, and this music which reduces material chaos to its basic components explains by a sort of grandiose mathematics how Nature orders and directs the birth of forms she draws from chaos.[36]

In these words the "Fibonacci Curve" is repostulated in another and occult language. Furthermore, this is where the yearned-for order of that curve meshes with the dread disorder—and endless possibility—of the desert or void, in the eyes of the poet and magician. This is the zone of hope and peril. This is the world of Yves Tanguy—his horizonless *Aux Jours de Lenteur* (Fig. 60), and his cyclonic *On Sonne* (Fig. 61). This is where Max Ernst's "eye of silence" (Fig. 62) broods at the hinterland of desert and labyrinth.

It was through peyote and its role in the rituals of the Tarahumara Indians that Artaud was made one with this

60. Yves Tanguy, *Aux Jours de Lenteur*, 1937. Oil on canvas. Musée National d'Art Moderne, Paris. Photo Bulloz.

61. Yves Tanguy, *On Sonne*, 1927. Oil on canvas. Galerie du Dragon, Paris.

62. Max Ernst, *The Eye of Silence*, 1943–44. Oil on canvas. Washington University, St. Louis, Mo. Photo Piaget.

landscape and this magic and was reborn—though, as was inevitable, reborn into another death:

They had lain me down on the very ground, at the foot of this enormous beam on which the three sorcerers sat, between one dance and another.

Lain me down low, so that the rite would descend upon me, so that fire, chants, cries, the dance and the very night might revolve like an animate human vault over me. So there was this rolling vault, this material ordering of howls, tones, footsteps, chants. But above all, beyond all, this impression, which recurred, that behind all that, more than that, and beyond it, still something else was hidden: the *principle*.

I did not renounce all at once these dangerous disassociations it seems Peyote provokes, and which I had sought for twenty years by other means: I did not mount on horseback with a body torn from itself and whose self-imposed privations would henceforth deprive it of its essential reflexes; I had not been this man of stone whom it took two men to make into a man on horseback, and whom they hoisted on and off my horse like a broken robot. . . . I had not conquered by force of spirit this invincible organic hostility, where it was *me* who no longer wanted to go on, in order to bring back from it a collection of dated imagery, from which this Age, so faithful to a whole system, would at the very most get a few new ideas for posters and models for its fashion designers. From now on it was necessary for the something buried behind this crushing trituration, which equates the dawn and the night, to be drawn out in the open and put to *use*, to serve precisely for *my crucifixion*.

To this, I knew my physical destiny was irremediably attached. I was ready for every burning and I waited the first fruits of burning, in view of a soon-to-be generalized combustion.[37]

There could have been no protection, no "precinct" of magical protection to punctuate the void. The self and non-self were exposed to the illimitable desert without a mandala or closed circle or architecture of defense. To the contrary, Don Juan took his bewildered Castaneda to witness another sorcerer, Don Genaro, perform impossible and inhuman leaps about a waterfall—in that same wilderness—under a powerful protection of magical will. And Castaneda asserted:

Don Juan then explained Don Genaro's feat. He said that he had already told me that human beings were, for those who "saw," luminous beings composed of something like fibres of light, which rotated from the front to the back and maintained the appearance of an egg. He said that he had also told me that the most astonishing part of the egg-like creatures was a set of long fibres that came out of the area around the navel; Don Juan said that those fibres were of the uttermost importance in the life of a man. Those fibres were the secret of Don Genaro's balance and his lesson had nothing to do with acrobatic jumps across the waterfall. His feat of equilibrium was in the way he used those "tentacle-like" fibres.[38]

At this point one begins to see how the non-self interfuses with the real self—the self beneath appearances and divisions —the self which glimpses its own nature as a fragment of Oneness, and which in so doing becomes able to perceive another, subliminal reality. By odd coincidence, Joan Miró, in 1928, painted three versions of a *Dutch Interior* in which Don Juan's world and even his description of man as truly *seen* are vivified. The point of departure for these remarkable presences was Dutch genre painting, discovered by Miró on a trip to Holland (Fig. 63). Miró takes a detailed "scene," the nuts-and-bolts stuff of anecdote and description, and *sees* a magical equation (Figs. 64–66). The theme is transported to another dimension. The egg-like presence with its fibrous tentacles appears. A fluid universe of light is evoked. An imagined footprint becomes a tangible entity. A bat and a frog emerge from nowhere. The tiled floor loses its status as a mere matter of fact and becomes a hallucinatory astonishment, just as in Huxley's drug experience. The fluid, circular preeminence of Schwenk's liquid universe and of the mystical mandalic zero become living laws yet again. Miró brings Don Juan's desert into the drawing room of European art. Against odds, he meshes an orgy of the supraconscious mind with the rigors of classicism. If André Breton, "high priest" of surrealism, chose to say that "Miró may rank as the most Surrealist of us all,"[39] it may well be true for this reason. Tanguy, Magritte, Delvaux, Dali tracked down the dream image with immense skill; Miró seizes it in midflight through the magic net of the inner eye.

We are dealing here with the seeming paradox of amazing precisions in a world of tenuous flux. So it is that the artist,

64. Joan Miró, *Dutch Interior I*, 1928. Oil on canvas, 36⅛" x 28¾". Collection, The Museum of Modern Art, N.Y. Mrs. Simon Guggenheim Fund.

65. Joan Miró, *Dutch Interior II*, 1928? Oil on canvas. Peggy Guggenheim Foundation, Venice.

66. Joan Miró, *Dutch Interior III*, 1928. Oil on canvas, 50¾" x 38". Private Collection.

the magician, and the magician-artist attempt to revolve and resolve the perimeter of the great circle.

The Occult Self

The desert of doubt and possibility abides always, and the labyrinths of protection—and explanation—maintain a delicate if indispensable position in its midst. The problem is that the self is never fixed or certain unless it hides within the labyrinth of the moment and pretends that those walls and dimensions encompass the whole of reality. If it does that, however, the end result is almost always a certain disillusionment, the sense that somehow, somewhere, in or outside of the coil of time, "there must be something else."

Everyone comes to this zero point at one time or another. The moment of cold reflection occupies some point along the screen or graph upon which one also finds an innocent young girl who dreams images of ancient subtlety and who symbolically prophecies her death, or a poet born to witness and annotate his destruction in an intolerable flame of life. Biological science proclaims the existence of junctures or gaps in the nervous system, called synapses. These calculated breaks in yet another continuous system serve to filter out an excess of sensation. Without them any semblance of order would be impossible. The result would be chaos. The mind would be inundated.

However, when those blessed limitations are altered, when slight modulations and certain increased capacities are effected, the results are marked by testimony which cannot be ignored. Any change in the capacity for reception indicates a change in the possibilities of interpretation and emission. A mind reconstituted is a cosmos reviewed. The tracings of such vision may sometimes be taken for madness—in which case they still cannot be quite ignored—or as inscriptions of genius —in which case they are frequently ignored. The usual technique is to attribute some middle ground of eccentric "imagination" or imaginative skill to the vision in order to disallow it as an intrinsic (scientific) observation of the nature of reality. The saint, magician, poet, or seer is allowed to plead *nolo contendere,* and so escape inquisition. The work of art then becomes a valuable object rather than a moral force, an exponent of its time rather than a landmark of timelessness.

Artaud, then, was in a unique position to see the suicide of Vincent Van Gogh as the *pietà* of modern art. It was a pure spiritual flame that Van Gogh sought and found, a rare access to inner, occult rhythms. It could not be tamed or contained. It amounted to a super-sanity. The sentence could not be commuted. Artaud observed:

Faced with the lucidity of Van Gogh at work, psychiatry becomes nothing but a cave of gorillas, themselves obsessed and persecuted, and who, to palliate the most frightful states of anguish and human suffocation, have only a ridiculous terminology . . . worthy product of their warped minds.

And he wrote:

Van Gogh did not die of a state of delirium proper but of having bodily been the field of a problem that the iniquitous spirit of mankind had debated since the beginning of time. That of the predominance of flesh over spirit, or body over flesh or of mind over one or the other.[40]

Later, Artaud added:

And where in this delirious thinking is there place for the human ego?
Van Gogh searched for his all his life, and with a strange energy and determination.
And he did not commit suicide in a fit of insanity, in terror of not succeeding, but to the contrary, he had just succeeded and had just discovered what he was and who he was, when the collective conscience of society, in order to punish him for tearing himself away from it, suicided him.[41]

Here, Artaud touches the nerve, the crucial point in regard to the poet-magician. Art history teaches that a given self or personality, under the influence of certain events or conditions, learns to transmute itself into art through interpretation and revelation and increased skill. Artaud's analysis suggests the very opposite. It suggests that those occult energies that lend art its life force precede the maker. Van Gogh becomes the "field of a problem" set by man's opposition to material illusions. He was actually able to paint that "field" in the magnetic flame-energy of his portraits (Fig. 67) and Provençal pastures (Figs 68–70). The force is brilliantly solar, and also richly cthonic—coming in its power from the guts of the earth as well. It is mirrored in the turbulent heat of the sun—the solar Zero—itself (Fig. 71), and even in such a microcosm as a section of fossilized palm (Figs. 72a, 72b).

So it was that a poetry or a knowledge or, better still, a *power* of light preceded Rembrandt van Rijn. Rembrandt becomes the medium, albeit the intelligent and active medium, of that power. He is the officiating priest of a divine *way*, but a priest who must paradoxically reinvent the preexisting order he serves, for the way must be eternally renewed within the time-stream to preserve its timelessness. He must be suf-

67. Vincent Van Gogh, *Self-Portrait*, 1889. Oil on canvas. Musée du Louvre, Paris. Photo Bulloz.

68. Vincent Van Gogh, *Olive Trees*, 1889. Oil on canvas. National Gallery of Scotland, Edinburgh. Annan Photographer, Glasgow.

69. Vincent Van Gogh, *Wheatfield with Reaper*, 1889. Oil on canvas. Rijksmuseum Vincent Van Gogh, Amsterdam. Photo Bulloz.

70. Vincent Van Gogh, *Long Grass with Butterflies*, 1890? Oil on canvas. The National Gallery, London.

71. Solar Prominence, 132,000 miles high. Hale Observatories, California Institute of Technology.

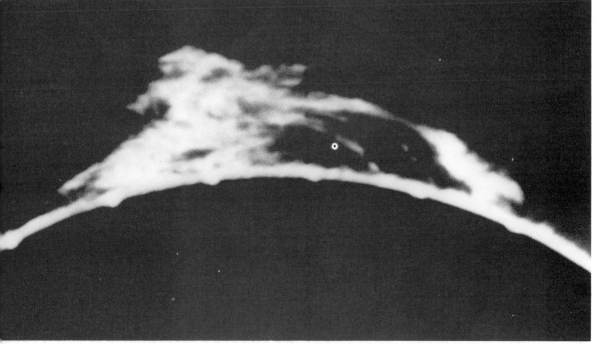

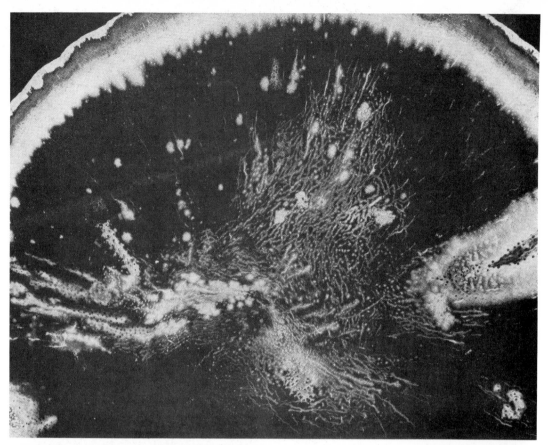

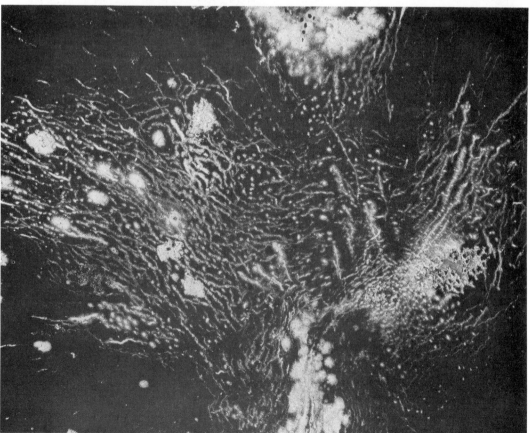

ficiently powerful to sustain and invoke those powers through the vessel of a singular human vision, and he must at the same time be prepared to relinquish his individuality—which is the way of any priest—though, as an artist, through annihilation rather than through anonymity. This is precisely what happened to Rembrandt, as to Van Gogh. Rembrandt did not take his own life, but he was none the less decimated by society in direct proportion to the attainment of his powers. In the early portraits, which were works of skill, the magic, the occult force, are not yet wholly apparent; society was well prepared to receive them. But the late protraits were rejected with what can be called a superstitious dread. And it is no accident that the greatest of these are the self-portraits. The image of the artist as Paul the Apostle (Fig. 73) acknowledges that Rembrandt had long since ceased to be an inventor or an interpreter and had become an apostle, a seer. In other versions the painter holds his brushes, barely seen save as vibrating presences within a glowing deepness of light (Fig. 74). At this point, as in Van Gogh's case (Fig. 75), they are more than symbols of his trade; they are very much the wand of the Magician, arcana I, come full circle to become the twin wands of arcana XXI, the World. In the Kenwood version Rembrandt is poised before two unexplained circles. The scholar J. G. van Gelder suggests that these are cabalistic symbols of God's perfection; in other words, the great Zero. J. A. Emmens prefers to see the ensemble in terms of Rembrandt mediating between "theory" and "practice"; which can be immediately translated as *thought* and *action*, or as the Fool and the Devil.

Light is the great key. In 1943, surrounded by the devastation of civilized Europe, Jean Cocteau was moved to write *The Myth of El Greco*. This short text proved to be a masterpiece of criticism and a rare perception of the occult force in art. He began:

Under the name of El Greco, Domenico Theotocopoulos passed live into mythology.

Was he not born in Crete, place of myth, where the man with the bull's torso beat his curly head against the walls of the labyrinth? And since the painter's mythology permits all audacities, should we not like to imagine him as born in the labyrinth

73. Rembrandt van Rijn, *Self Portrait as the Apostle Paul*, 1661. Oil on canvas. Rijksmuseum, Amsterdam.

74. Rembrandt van Rijn, *Portrait of the Artist*, 1663? Oil on canvas. Iveagh Bequest, Kenwood House, London.

75. Vincent van Gogh, *Self-Portrait*, 1888. Oil on canvas. Private collection. Photo Bulloz, Paris.

and growing longer until he incarnates his shadow, in order to flee his geometric jail for a sky peopled with a chaos of wings and clothes which twist and tear, and rays of light (Fig. 76).

From the labyrinth of Crete, a real prefiguration of the plan of Toledo, he went to the labyrinth of Venice where outlines elongated and tormented in the water no doubt enriched him more than the school of Titian and Tintoretto.

In these few words alone we have the labyrinth and the void, the creative media of water and air, the hallucinatory reality, the opposition of the occult self to the material self. And at the end of his essay, Cocteau reflected upon another dimension:

On re-reading these lines it appears to me that I have been caught by the exalted rhythm of El Greco and have not expatiated sufficiently on the painter he was as such, as well as being a great figure of mystical initiation.

The case is so exceptional that it would be unjust not to take it into account. In fact it often happens that an artist preoccupied with problems of an occult order expresses himself more through the spirit than through matter and that the artist preoccupied with matter often neglects the spirit and only seeks to resolve problems of a pictorial nature. With El Greco we witness this miracle: a painter who "fingers matter" like Velasquez and puts his strength as an artisan in the service of the mind.[42]

This issue—the fusion of mind and flesh—is one of the most crucial and most delicate in the magician's repertory. Any artist knows that the two are one, that mind is not the brain alone but the entire sensate composite of soma which forms the senses and participates in the miracle of awareness. So that the body is itself a labyrinth which encloses, imprisons, and protects the mind—while it is simultaneously a refraction or particle of the void, the desert, that cosmic energy which is Mind itself.

One often speaks, without thinking of any occult implications, of "an inner life." A person transported by rage is described as being "beside himself." And the word "soul" is still used to describe a certain elusive but ineluctable reality. Those who have ever practiced yoga or meditation know that the stillness of the unconscious is a channel to modes of receptivity inaccessible to the inductive mind. All of which

makes it slightly easier to approach the occultist's view of the human being as consisting of three successive sheaths of self: the material body, the etheric body, and the astral body. The first is the molecular husk which we can see, and which suffers under the whine of the dentist's drill. The second is a much finer, more luminous understructure of spirit, a connection between singularity and cosmic energy, between the one and the great Zero. The third and innermost is pure spirit, pure soul. Yet this layer too somehow possesses the attributes of the self. It may be more appropriate, in accordance with the designations of the Tarot mentioned earlier, to begin instead at the center. The astral body would be associated with the eternal Zero, the etheric body with the one of Oneness $(I = 0)$, and the physical body with the two of forms and divisions, the work and prey of Baphomet. We are told that the astral body yearns to leave its physical prison and, in some instances, manages to do so during sleep; if so, it is able to travel beyond physical limitations, always attached to its husk by an etheric cord.

There exists a self-portrait by Miró in which this interfusion of levels becomes amazingly visible (Fig. 77). It is all the more interesting that William Rubin's excellent description of this drawing does not come from any predetermination to associate it with the occult:

> In [an] earlier work . . . Miró gives us but a skin-deep self-image, whereas in the later he has rendered himself transparent. From out of the contours of his features emerges the universe of his imagination. His liberated line has woven a galactic tracery of sparks, flames, suns, and stars. . . . This astral conflagration seems to begin in the incandescent eyes and to pass with an incendiary rapidity throughout the space of the image. The real features seem almost to dissolve into the swirling chiaroscuro, as if "all impurities (had) been burned away." What remains are *les étincelles*, the sparks of pure idea, the single cells from which *miromonde* grew, bodied forth in Miró's iconography through a variety of references to light—from a firefly to a sun to the shimmering of a thousand sardines.[43]

The word "astral" is used here in reference to the stars themselves, perhaps without direct allusion to any astral equivalence in the flesh; yet, the sense is very much intact.

77. Joan Miró, *Self-Portrait I*, 1937–38. Pencil, crayon, and oil on canvas, 57½" x 38¼". Collection, James Thrall Soby, New Caanan, Conn.

Blake's "eternity in a flower," the macrocosm in the microcosm, is the point. Miró has transfigured the flesh in a calligraphy of mind.

However, another key to this passage lies in its equivalence of light and speed, or time. The light of Miró-World, firefly or sun—this "astral conflagration" (a phrase Artaud would have understood)—passes through the image "with an incendiary rapidity." Such a flame creates or destroys, and here the reference is to the speed of *light*. Now the speed of light (186,000 miles per second), as physics testifies, is the physical perimeter of human existence. It is a bewildering canon that man in the body can never travel faster than the speed of light despite any possible feats of technology. Jets may break the sound barrier by far, but any vessel that might equal the speed of light would automatically equal in density the mass of the entire universe. The idea is scarcely graspable. It means that to surpass the speed of light in physical terms would mean the reaching of infinity and, at the same time, annihilation. In terms of the Tarot this would mean absorption into the great Zero. There would be no access to modulation, to form, to the divisions of Behemoth; there would be no shield against the most dazzling of lights, no recall from total darkness. One's biology would cease, one's physiology would disappear. Mind, in our limited, human sense would vanish. There would be only the undifferentiated Zero.

Fortunately, then, Miró's "incendiary rapidity" is much short of that ultimate implosion. On the other hand, it is relatively quicker than most other modes of vision. (The fact that "quick" means both *rapid* and *alive* is more than coincidence.)

After Rutherford proved that the atom is basically energy rather than mass, and in keeping with Einstein's reflection that in the light of energy all is relative, Max Planck showed, in his Quantum Theory, that light and speed are intertwined, as lovers.

In his day, Goya was accused of graphic inaccuracies in his drawings of bulls of the *corrida*. Only later, with the invention of photography, were his observations proved correct. His eye was capable of "stopping" motion with the fractional speed of a modern shutter. The fact, however, would be a crude illustration of the *speed of vision* were it not for the rate at which Goya's optic was capable of transcribing apparent stillness: in the portraits (Fig. 78). In *Gulliver's Travels*, a work so cosmic in perception that children find it easier to understand than adults, Jonathan Swift relates how the Emperor of Lilliput was able to see the movement of the clock's minute hand. So was Goya able to see the motion, the active life, the inner life and luminosity of his "subject." He saw beneath the physical body. And the vision reached so strenuously into his able flesh that he was even able to transcribe it.

Was this because Goya was greatly more "skilled" than Jean Auguste Dominique Ingres? Hardly. The only difference between them—that is, the universe of difference—lay in their *speed of vision*. Ingres could not paint a length of silk that was not erotic; as a surgeon of sensuality he was probably unequalled in the history of art; neither Courbet nor Manet, nor Delacroix nor Toulouse-Lautrec ever approached the flesh with such ingenious brutality. Their aims were elsewhere. They wanted to transcend the flesh, and they succeeded; whereas Ingres abides *in flagrento delecti* in art history. He is the master of the physical or material body—even when his nudes are fully clothed (Fig. 79).

It is just that Goya's eye moved at another perceptual speed—even as it moves at still another rate from that of El Greco. The latter painted a human flame, the sort of flame that is invisible in sunlight, writhing, in a helix, free of its physical prison. In other words, he painted the astral body. Ingres caressed and expatiated the flesh with a bold intimacy that skirts obscenity in the way a torero flirts with the bull he is about to slaughter. In other words, he painted the material body. But Goya found an illumination that is not quite divine and not quite human, that stands anthropoid upon the ground and reaches up into the light until it seems to become light itself. In this, he was equalled perhaps only by Rembrandt. Each of them reached into the etheric body. There are no references to style or even to mysticism that offer an explanation of how this came about. The modes of El Greco's genius are miraculous, but one can discuss them in terms of spirit. In the Paris of 1943 this tormented and

78. Francisco Goya, *Portrait of the Marquesa de Solana*, 18th C. Oil on canvas. Musée du Louvre, Paris. Photo Bulloz.

79. Jean Auguste Dominique Ingres, *Grande Odalisque* (detail), 1814. Oil on canvas. Musée du Louvre, Paris, Photo Bulloz.

sublime freedom must have been irresistible to Cocteau—and so it always is, and so it increasingly becomes. Yet Rembrandt and Goya never relinquished the proximity of flesh. Their speed of vision took in the poise of the body just as it acknowledged the supremacy of light. This is the etheric plane. And it cannot be sustained. Rembrandt tuned his light into an overwhelming silence. Goya went on into his "Black" paintings. The "real" world no longer sufficed. He went on into the world of wholly occult vocabulary—of demons, of presences, of premonitions. The man who had etched *The Disasters of War* with a cold passion now painted the faces of Behemoth without apology to a world ignorant of its own spiritual anatomy. But these last paintings were no more occult than their predecessors, for all that. Perhaps less. In the faces of an ordinary royal family of uncertain eyes and weak jaws, Goya had transcribed the energies of creation. In the spectacle of witches, demons, and black sabbaths, he painted the hideous reflection of what men call reality.

The Magical Self

Odd similarities exist between Goya and Beethoven. They looked remarkably alike; they were akin in "symphonic" temperament; they worked in dark and voluminous harmonies; in their time they looked to Bonaparte with hope, and then turned their genius against the usurper: Beethoven in the *Eroica* Symphony, Goya in *The Disasters of War*; both continued to grow in psychic or creative power after their physical frames began to fail lamentably. Beethoven was deaf when, in an act of dynamic will, he tried to conduct his greatest masterpiece, the Ninth Symphony; and Goya wrote at eighty-two, "I can't see or write or hear—I have nothing left but the will—and that I have in abundance." [44]

It is a long way from these European giants of ego back to the hieratic gods of Mexico; still, we have heard Don Juan speak of will as the agent of power and invulnerability.

This energy, which streams up from a source beyond the ego, is central to art and magic; this will is manifest. It is an extension of the hope common to all survivors of daily peril (despair), just as the psychic's clairvoyant power is an extension of a keen intuition. Yet it rises onto another plane. And when the self allows its will to do so, the will automatically assumes yet another power or dimension. For this reason, the poet or magician has the sensation of being forever on the threshold of a further illumination. His impression is always one of relative inadequacy. Whereupon he sinks into what he assumes to be despair, and rises—always astonished—into a new consciousness. His self, hopefully, is more autonomous than the perplexed self of Antonin Artaud; still, he knows himself to be a medium, the "field of a problem."

Will, like hope itself, exists independent of an object. Will exerts a certain magnetic field. It is part of the life force.

Therefore, whether it really *finds* its object, or whether the object attaches itself to the will by virtue of the same magnetism is indeterminable. The point is that the two find each other. When they do, will and its object form the center of a new mandala. The perimeter becomes the shape of a new being, a new art. It may be El Greco or Van Gogh or Goya or even Ingres. However, by nature—if the word applies—the center is eternal (the will), and the perimeter is unimpeachable. Only the area between those points remains open to interpretation.

If Aleister Crowley proclaimed the doctrine, "Do What Thou Wilt Shall Be the Whole of the Law," that statement is all too easily open to misunderstanding. He meant a dramatically controlled species of will at the service of a Law that *will* alone can decipher. We have already mentioned the paradoxical role of the artist as a priest who must reinvent, within time, the way of timelessness which he serves. Crowley's sense is close to this; it reflects the ego of the poet at the service of the great supraegotistical Zero.

The life of Aleister Crowley has drawn varying degrees of praise and blame, but it has rarely been confronted in full perspective although our own anguished age ought to make that perspective somewhat easier to acknowledge. A magician of "plastic" works such as Max Ernst can be laureled as a maker of beauty, and so neutralized as a magical consciousness. But Crowley must ever remain a loose nerve end, a dangerous live wire, a worker of magical acts, a Nietzschean man. And yet these two magicians have more in common than criticism or biography are wont to acknowledge.

That Crowley is celebrated as a scarlet figure, a black magician of theatrical bent, cannot be put down to ill faith; it was the image he himself chose to create under the name of Master Therion, the Great Beast 666, mystical number of antichrist in the Book of Revelations. However, that profile was only half the geography of Crowley's mind. He was also a gifted poet of white magic. His dimensions were larger than life-size and, in fact, he fitted in with the Nietzschean ideal of will beyond the contours of all that is "human, all too human." This need not be evil at all. Nietzsche had written in *Thus Spake Zarathustra:*

But tell me, my brothers, what can the child do that even the lion cannot? Why must the preying lion become a child?

The child is innocence and forgetfulness, a new beginning, a sport, a self-propelling wheel, a first motion, a sacred Yes.

Yes, a sacred Yes is needed, my brothers, for the sport of creation; the spirit now wills *its own* will, the spirit now sundered from the world now wins *its own* world.[45]

The question of will is inescapable for every architect of the desert. However, whereas Nietzsche only recognized the sacred will of a romantically and nebulously defined "superman," Crowley laid claim to the help of higher agencies and underlying law, diabolical or otherwise. In terms of ever active balance upon the great wheel, in the undercurrents of the Fool and Behemoth, his case is unique.

It may be that the first death of Crowley's limited self occurred at the age of fifteen, when he tried to light a bomb on Guy Fawkes Night and was unconscious for over three days. Accidents have been known to suddenly awaken psychic potential for the first time. The mind is jogged off course, like a celestial body torn out of orbit and turned maverick in space.

From the day when, at fourteen, he seduced the maid on his mother's bed, Crowley's sexual powers were central to a staggering career. As of the accident, he was able to speak of a "jungle sensitiveness" which served infallibly in his favorite sport of mountain climbing as in his dealings with mankind, and especially womankind. But it was his meeting with MacGregor Mathers of the Order of the Golden Dawn that technically launched his career in magic.

The name MacGregor was an acquisition, his real name being Samuel Liddell Mathers; for he too was a creation of Celtic spirit. He had discovered *The Book of the Sacred Magic of Abra-Melin the Mage* in a Paris library, and this work served as one of Crowley's advanced primers while he was a neophyte of the spirits.

Crowley's biographer, John Symonds, explains that:

Abraham the Jew (or his Master, Abra-Melin) seems to have been an honest man. His magic does not explain one mystery by another, but is a kind of teach-yourself system in which some practical guidance is given for those who wish to impose their will on nature. Since contemplation, prayer, and abstinence are enjoined, the magic of the Mage who called himself Abra-Melin is, in essence, the same as that Eastern magic commonly known as yoga. For this reason, perhaps, it works.[46]

It must be emphasized that the work teaches the superiority of good forces over bad, of white over black magic. It commands six months active preparation in that birthplace of poets and magi, the wilderness. It asserts that man occupies a middle position between a Holy Guardian Angel and a Malevolent Demon; that if the seeker applies himself and succeeds, his Angel will appear in radiance to acknowledge and command, but that if he fails the demon will instead conquer, destroy, and possess.

Crowley immediately chose London as his wilderness, and hardly proceeded to follow Abra-Melin to the letter. In place of the requisite humility he adopted what would be the first of many disguises, and passed himself off grandly as Count Vladimir Svareff. He also fitted up two of his rooms as goetic temples—one devoted to white magic and the other to the black variety.

This duality marks the whole of Crowley's career and constitutes what may be its most fascinating element. In the *Book of Thoth*, *The Heart of The Master*, *The Dangers of Mysticism*, and his one novel, *Moonchild*, he espouses the way of white magic and assumes the role of white magician. He thus fulfilled one of the dicta set down by Nietzsche at the beginning of *Twilight of the Idols*: "I mistrust all systematizers and avoid them. The will to a system is a lack of integrity." [47] True, Crowley would all his life codify laws and rituals, and command with the angry voice of the prophet, but he also eschewed the shallows of consistency in favor of what a "jungle sensitiveness" dictated in terms of revelation and will. That he managed to command possession of this ability is the key to his magic, its black diabolism and white reverence.

He wrote from New York to a young neophyte disciple in Vancouver suggesting certain applications of ritual and advised that:

The time is just ripe for a natural religion. . . . Insist on the real benefits of the Sun, the Mother-Force, the Father-Force and so on; and show that by celebrating these benefits worthily the worshippers unite themselves more fully with the current of life. Let the religion be Joy, with but a worthy and dignified sorrow in death itself; and treat death as an ordeal, an initiation. Do not gloss over facts, but transmute them in the Anthenor of your ecstasy. In short be the founder of a new and greater Pagan cult. . . . As you go on you can add new festivals of corn and wine, and all things useful and noble and inspiring.[48]

The sense and the tone might almost be that of D. H. Lawrence in a moment of redemptive inspiration. But, as always, there were two sides of the story: the word *anthanor* normally refers to an alchemist's furnace; yet according to the secret code employed by Crowley and the O.T.O. (*Ordo Templi Orientis*) it really meant the penis—just as the retort or the *cucurbite* stood for the vagina, and the Serpent or the *blood of the red lion* for the semen. These substitutions had been adopted, at least in part, to circumvent the censorship of the Edwardian period.

The O.T.O. had been founded in Germany early in the century. It was basically a Masonic order with fallacious claims to a direct ancient lineage, and apparently plausible claims to the revelation of all Masonic secrets. The catch was that those "unutterable" secrets cannot be uttered, and are valueless without the application of magic. This was where Crowley excelled. He quickly rose in the scale of initiation from the I° to the VIII° and IX°. These last degrees were devoted to sexual magic. Crowley was in process of mastering them at precisely the period in which he wrote so idyllically to Vancouver. In *The Magical Record of the Beast 666* he lists his lunar minions. Among them:

Margaret Pitcher. A young, pretty stupid, wide-mouthed, flat-faced, slim-bodied harlot. Fair hair. Fine fat juicy Yoni.
  Viola. Hideous taurine doped prostitute.
  Helen Marshall. Irish-American prostitute. Taurus rising. Beautiful lazy type. Not actually passionate or perverse. A cheerful comfortable girl.[49]

Symonds comments, "He was at this period also sodomised by two strangers in a Turkish bath in New York, and he practised fellatio with a third, all on the same night; they were acts for a magic purpose for he rarely indulged in sex for the mere pleasure of it." [50]

This would appear true. The ladies mentioned above were not the great scarlet women of his career, only bit players on the altar of magic. In contrast, he converted a Pennsylvania Dutch girl into his service as Whore of the Stars, alias the Dog. She, in turn, was succeeded by the Camel, so named because she helped him cross the desert of spiritual peril. And throughout he worked at drawing up and refining the occult formulae and rituals of the scholar-mage, with deference to the laws of the Kabala, the wisdom of the Tarot, the tenets of the O.T.O., and, with increasing frequency, the promptings of The Lady of Dreams—opium. It was in 1918 that he met Alma Hersig, whom he renamed Leah and installed as The Scarlet Woman and The Great Ape of Thoth—his principal lunar accomplice on as near a permanent basis as the Beast found possible.

During the war years Crowley managed to complicate matters still further by writing anti-English invective for a pro-German magazine called *The Fatherland*—as a result of a chance meeting with one of its staff on a Fifth Avenue bus. If the affair was treasonous it was also absurd. He complained that his aunt's house had been spared in a bombing of Croydon, and furnished Count Zeppelin the exact address. Later he claimed the Victoria Cross for having sabotaged the Germans by the patent absurdity of his claims. The entire episode was tawdry and also silly, but it only underscores the fact that not only did Crowley have no human sympathy for people, he properly speaking had no self in the usual sense either. In diablery and in piety, in sodomy and in prayer, sober or drugged, he was a terrible eye, a cold lunar consciousness loose upon the world.

It is perhaps that lack of self that made his energy apparently superhuman or at least larger than life-size. The first of the Nietzschean *Maxims and Arrows* proclaims: "Idleness is the beginning of all psychology. What? Could psychology be—a vice?" [51] Crowley's case could well have been the mirror image of that—the lack of human psychology may have banished all idleness. In any case, merely to read the record of the man's travels and labors and learnings and possessions and defilements and enchantments is exhausting.

What he had found was a wellspring of form-energy and

the power to invoke it. Are the essentially pagan gargoyles of Notre Dame de Paris (Fig. 80) any more good or evil than the "abstract" gargoyle carved by Jean Arp (Fig. 81) over half a millennium later? Blake's Behemoth (Fig. 82), adapted from the Book of Job, is no less a part of the cosmic spiral than the Behemoth of the Tarot. Bosch and Brueghel, whatever their conclusions may have been, painted their demons as manifestations of light and darkness seized by the inner eye (Figs. 83, 84). This was Crowley's sense. He ascended and descended the spiral, sometimes in both directions at once. And like Max Ernst (Fig. 85), he drew these daunting presences into the salons of Europe and America.

His travels spread as far as Africa and California, Sicily and Mexico—where 666 reported the highly symbolic as well as occult act of making his image disappear in a mirror. The degree of scholarly devotion was profound as well as profuse, and became concrete in a plethora of published works. In addition to all else, Crowley, when not given over to bombast, wrote well. As indicated, the number of omnisexual liaisons was bewildering. On their return to Europe, it was the Great Ape herself who manually assisted the Beast in performing

80. Gargoyles, Notre Dame de Paris. 12th–13th C. Photo Bulloz.

81. Jean Arp, *Gargoyle*, 1949. Sandstone. Private collection.

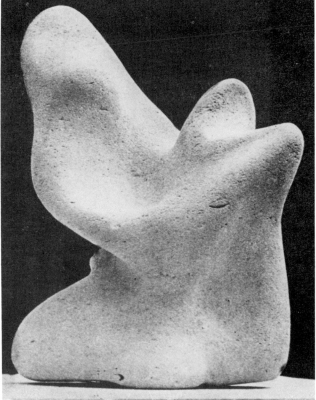

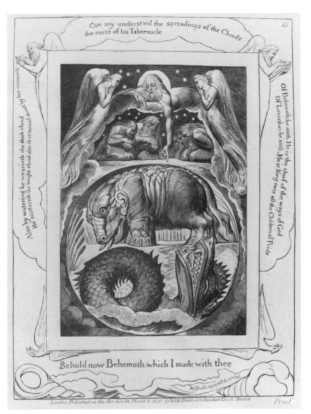

82. William Blake, *The Book of Job*, 1825. Engraving (plate XV). The British Museum.

83. Hieronymus Bosch, *The Temptation of St. Anthony* c. 1500 (detail). Panel of triptych. National Museum, Lisbon. Photo Bulloz, Paris.

84. Pieter Brueghel the elder, *Fall of the Rebel Angels*, 1562. Oil on canvas. Musées Royeaux des Beaux Arts, Brussels. Photo Bulloz, Paris.

85. Max Ernst, *Fire*, from *Une Semaine de Bonté*, 1934. Collage. Bibliothèque Nationale. Photo Giraudon.

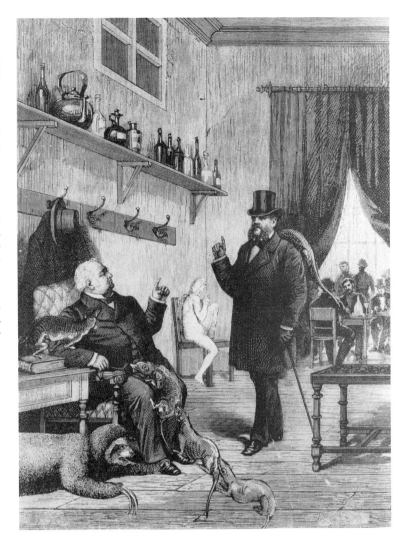

his homosexual rites. She also bore his child and reigned over his Sicilian temple, the famous Abbey of Thelema—the Greek word for will. For Freud the sexual organ was the center of the universe; for Crowley it was merely the key to eternity.

Then there was the fiend opium, an all-devouring habit which Crowley nonetheless managed to beat and make the subject of a long, highly original book. And at the end, gin. Crowley died in 1954, and I have myself met an English lady who claims to have been abducted by him when she was two, made to undress and worship the sun. No harm seems to have occurred, but it should be added that the lady is today a practicing witch—a white witch.

The Magical Self   91

It was also in America, in 1917, that Crowley found time to produce his only novel, *Moonchild*. Its theme is that ancient occult obsession, the creation of a lunar, godlike, mythological child in this world, through magic. In the telling of it, Crowley plays wholly the role of the white magician and, with straight-faced piety, mantles his ex-associates of the Golden Dawn, including Yeats, in evil.

He even goes so far as to portray himself as a young apprentice magician, Cyril Gray, a man of awed humility as well as of intense good. His master, however, called Simon Iff, is the projection of Crowley as an old man, as a master among masters. Cyril asks Simon Iff his secret of protection against occult danger. Iff replies:

"To have assimilated all things so perfectly that there is no longer any possibility of a struggle. To have destroyed the idea of duality. To have achieved Love and Will so that there is no longer any object to Love, or any aim for Will. To have killed desire at the root; to be one with everything and with Nothing.

"Look!" he went on, with a change of tone, "why does a man die when he is struck by lightning? Because he has a gate open to lightning; he insists on being an electrical substance by possessing the quality of resistance to the passage of the electric current. If we could diminish that resistance to zero, lightning would no longer take notice of him.

"There are two ways of preventing a rise of temperature from the sun's heat. One is to oppose a shield of nonconducting and opaque material: that is Cyril's way, and at best it is imperfect; some heat always gets through. The other is to remove every particle of matter from the space you wish to be cold; then there is nothing there to become hot; and that is the way of the Tao." [52]

He also adds, to the lady who is to bear the moonchild, "It would mean giving up yourself . . . and you'll have to do it one day." The passage says much about Crowley at his height. It says much to apply focus to what an outsider may see as merely outrageous or as hypocrisy. Again, it touches upon the theme of self-creation twinned with annihilation, of magical or poetic birth consummated in the presence of destruction. The process occurs in very many ways, in proportion to the spiritual capacity of the bearer.

Here it must be pointed out that Crowley's understanding of the poetic act far outdistanced that of other modern occult figures. He may not have been the poet he thought himself to be; still, his sonnet in praise of Rodin's *Balzac* (Fig. 86), written at a time when the sculpture was under violent attack, was translated into French by no less a *littérateur* than Marcel Schwob. And Crowley's words acutely identified the masterpiece as the embodiment not of a physical person but of a fountainhead of creative energy. The poem also led to Crowley's meeting with Rodin:

86. Auguste Rodin, *Balzac*, 1898 (detail). Plaster. Photo Giraudon.

Rodin told me how he had conceived his Balzac. He had armed himself with all the documents; and they had reduced him to despair. (Let me say at once that Rodin was not a man, but a god. He had no intellect in the true sense of the word; his was a virility so superabundant that it constantly overflowed into the creation of vibrating visions. . . .)

He was seized with a sort of rage of destruction, abandoned his pathetically pedantic programme. Filled with the sublime synthesis of the data which had failed to convey a concrete impression to his mind, he set to work and produced the existing Balzac. This consequently bore no relation to. the incidents of Balzac's personal appearance at any given period. These things are only veils. Shakespeare would still have been Shakespeare if someone had thrown sulphuric acid in his face. The real Balzac is the writer of the *Comédie Humaine*; and what Rodin had done is to suggest this spiritual abstraction through the medium of form.

The analysis is quite perfect. Then Crowley recalls an incident that occurred in Rodin's studio:

Some bright spirit had brought his fiddle and we were all bewitched. Rodin suddenly smiled and waved his hand towards "Pan et Syrinx." I followed the gesture: The bars just played were identical with the curve of the jaw of the girl. *The power to perceive such identities of essence beneath a difference of material manifestation is the inevitable token of mastery.*[53] [Italics mine.]

In these words Crowley not only caresses the sense of Rodin's art but touches upon the occult dimension of all art. Beneath any "material manifestation," Rodin's massive *Balzac* twists and turns in a thrust of energy visibly parallel to Schwenk's photographs of water behaving as it must. The *image* is *organic*. *Ecclesiastes* says: "Who knoweth the spirit of man that goeth upward, and the spirit of the beast that goeth downward to the earth?" which is an expression of the same helix or spiral.

Still, here we have the artist stretched on that spiral between the Fool and the Devil. There is a passage in Crowley's *Confessions*, set down at a moment of high intensity—while ascending to the IX°, and transferring his attention from the Snake to the Cat—that speaks vividly:

The word of a Magus is always a falsehood. For it is a creative word; there would be no object in uttering it if it merely stated an existing fact in nature. The task of a Magus is to make his word, the expression of his will, come true. It is the most formidable labour that the mind can conceive.[54]

This is not far from the point Oscar Wilde had made in *The Art of Lying*—that the artist does not reveal a preexisting truth but in fact creates that truth, in contradiction of visible nature but in keeping with inner, underlying harmonies. He stated that if one passes the Green Park in the heart of London after having seen an exhibition of Japanese landscape painting, the foliage, the mists, the tonalities, all become totally Japanese. The mind creates and reforms nature. And like Crowley, Wilde tried to join the higher and lower as One, to adopt the way of "Do what thou wilt" based upon an aesthetic and somewhat mystical reverence. It was a battle for perfection of soul, a supersoul, amid the fragments of time and matter and circumstance. The failure is recorded not only in the tragic retrospective of *De Profundis* but even presaged in *The Portrait of Dorian Gray*, where the increasingly hideous portrait of the "true" soul of the ageless Dorian testifies to an insuperable division of the higher and the lower. In the end, Wilde himself chose to accept martyrdom, to finish his life in a veil of expiation.

Whereas Crowley, even as his body tottered and disintegrated, and gin took its final toll, continued to beat his wings against time and pursue a godlike vision of Oneness. The great agony, in magus or poet, is that of somehow sustaining the magic moment, the clarity, of suspending timelessness in time. The fusion of *light* and *life* is the act of consummate peril. Lawrence wrote towards the end:

I have been defeated and dragged down by pain
and worsted by the evil world-soul of today.
But still I know that life is for delight
and for bliss
as now when the tiny wavelets of the sea
tip the morning light on edge, and spill it with delight
to show how inexhaustible it is.

Life is for kissing and for horrid strife,
the angels and the Sunderers.
And perhaps in unknown Death we perhaps shall know
Oneness and poised immunity.
But why then should we die while we can live?

And while we live
the kissing and communing cannot cease
nor yet the striving and the horrid strife.[55]

So he linked the angels and the Sunderers, and capitalized the latter. It was he who had written a couplet called "Retort to Jesus":

And whoever forces himself to love anybody
begets a murderer in his own body.[56]

Do what you wilt. . . . Yet there is no calculating the extent of the sacrifice once the self, the "too, too solid flesh," begins to slip into Oneness. These acrobatics of the spirit demand a singleness of nerve. It was the fire of war that ignited Max Ernst's goetic consciousness. He wrote of himself—significantly, in the third person, as Henry Adams had done—as the self regarding the self:

Max Ernst died on 1st August, 1914. He returned to life on 11th November, 1918, a young man who wanted to become a magician and find the central myth of his age. From time to time he consulted the eagle which had guarded the egg of his prenatal existence. The bird's advice can be detected in his work.[57]

Ernst had always been in the path of magic, however, as his recollections show. Again, the proximity of sudden death altered the light of vision:

(1897) First contact with the void: his sister Maria kissed him and her sister goodbye and died a few hours later. Since this time, a feeling for Nothingness and destructive forces has been dominant in his temperament, in his behaviour, and—later—in his work. . . .
(1906) First contact with occult and magical powers. One of his best friends, a highly intelligent and devoted pink cockatoo, died on the night of 5th January. It was a fearful shock to Max when he found the dead bird next morning, at the same instant as his father informed him of the birth of his sister Lori. . . . In his imagination he connected the two events and blamed the baby for the bird's decease. . . .
Excursions into the world of prodigies, chimaeras, phantoms, poets, monsters, philosophers, birds, women, madmen, magi, trees, erotica, stones, insects, mountains, poisons, mathematics, etc.[58]

Out of these origins the texture and shape and shadow of perceived reality acquired a universe of meaning, innuendo, hope, and menace—in short, of life. The Freudian mechanician would probably read Ernst's words as a confession in which a succession of neurotic associations follow a childhood trauma. The Jungian point of view, however, would be quite the reverse: a lightning flash during childhood awakens Ernst's mind to a universe of archetypal possibilities. A new *luminosity* is created, through which vision becomes a *creative* force. A qualitative elevation of *will* takes place. A magician is born.

As in the case of Crowley, the sexual conundrum is rarely absent. In 1923, he painted a cosmology related to this theme with the pointed title, *Of This Men Shall Know Nothing* (Fig. 87). The upper portion celebrates female sexuality, the lower portion deals with the male. As part of an inscription drawn on the back of the picture, Ernst commented:

87. Max Ernst, *Of This Men Shall Know Nothing*, 1923. Oil on canvas. Tate Gallery, London.

The hand shields the Earth. This movement endows the Earth with the significance of a sexual organ.

The moon goes at great speed through its phases and eclipses.

The picture is unusual in its symmetry. The two sexes maintain each other in a state of balance.

Still, there is a definite suggestion of the male element being acted upon by the female, the former as terrestrial, the latter as celestial. Again, the great Zero encapsulates all.

The Moon Goddess, the White Goddess

In the pantheon of occult vision the female presence is seen as a lunar force, the male function as solar. Here one must return to the Tarot. For the Devil in the avatar of Behemoth is a clearly androgynous figure, possessing the arms and breasts of a female, the legs and sex of a male. Just as in Ernst's painting, the upper is female, the lower is male; but the two are one. So are the sun and moon the twin symbols of inclusive energy. They represent polarities that are part of a whole. Literature reflects this male-female equilibrium as a great solution and a great enigma. Astronomically, the sun is the great sustaining force of life, and the moon regulates the tides and establishes biological rhythms. Instinctively at least, we regard the sexual union-division as a fulcrum of harmony and discord.

The potent arcana XVIII and XIX are devoted respectively to the Moon and the Sun. Before viewing them directly, however, one must make note of the zone in which the Devil is situated. The Fool, as we have seen, reigns between arc. I, the Magician, and arc. XXI, the World. In turn, the Devil is poised between the fourteenth key, which the French call *La Tempérance* (Fig. 88), and the sixteenth, the Tower, called in France *La Maison de Dieu* (Fig. 89).

The word *temperance* denotes moderation but also, through its French root, refers to time. In any case, there is an essential rhythm here, an equilibrium. The angelic figure is described by Crowley as androgynous, but by Wirth as gynandrous—or of doubtful sex. Its forehead bears the great zero in still another form; its hands transverse a liquid to and

88. Tarot: Arc. XIV, *La Tempérance* (Temperance, or Art). Woodcut, French, 1760.

89. Tarot: Arc. XVI, *La Maison Dieu* (The Tower). Woodcut, French, 1760.

from a vase of gold and a vase of silver. Wirth's interpretation of this symbol bears close attention:

The urns of precious metal do not correspond to coarse corporeal containers; they allude to the double physical atmosphere whose material organism is only a terrestrial vestige. Of these concentric auras, the nearer one is solar and active (Gold, consciousness, reason): it directs the individual in an immediate fashion and engages its voluntary energy. The other expands beyond the first; it is lunar and sensitive (Silver). Its domain is more mysterious; it is that of sentiment, of subtle impressions, of imagination and of a higher order of the subconscious. This etheric sphere englobes the life common to individuals of the same species, a continuous life from which we draw the life force which we then individualize. That which is concentrated in the silver urn flows into the gold urn, where its condensation is consummated in view of its contact with physical life.[59]

The attentive reader will immediately understand why Aleister Crowley chose to redefine arc. XIV as *Art* rather than as Temperance or Time. The very sense of the card lent it the underlying architecture of timelessness in the spirit.

Consider, then, the card installed at the other side of the Devil, arcana XVI, the Tower. This sigil of destruction represents the antithesis of Temperance. For purposes of divination it is the "worst" card in the pack; for all that, it was dear to William Butler Yeats whose knowledge of occult doctrine and whose sensitivity to mystical truth were among the most prodigious of our time. Yeats wrote of this dread sigil:

I declare this tower is my symbol; I declare
This winding, gyring, spiring treadmill of a star
is my ancestral stair . . .[60]

It is an odd allegiance; but then one realizes that Yeats chose a singularly lunar path in his life and work. He was an exquisite exponent of almost Proustian nostalgia in a Celtic key, of love and time lost. He lamented the dying flesh and mused wistfully upon youth. His particular sense of the great Oneness comes in opposition to the human frame:

For one throb of the artery,
While on that old grey stone I sat
Under the old wind-broken tree,
I knew that One is animate,
Mankind inanimate fantasy.[61]

So that Yeats, with his "tower, half dead at the top," was in fact only a partial agent of will. Which may help to explain, beyond all the stated controversies, his bitter clash with Crowley in the Golden Dawn—Crowley whose magic tended to be solar, phallic, entwined with the flesh. Thus, in *Moon-*

child, the fictionalized Yeats is rather maliciously portrayed as a bungler, annihilated by an invocation of the magical power of arcana XVI. Yeats lived to write, Crowley wrote out of an abundance of living. Crowley ended as the victim of the life-magic he once commanded, and Yeats died a hero of letters. Yet there is a certain melancholy to the triumph. He confronted Oneness as a gifted scribe. Crowley went headlong into the conflagration, consumed in Oneness as a magician.

As the great wheel sweeps upward towards its consummation, two mighty presences are brilliantly defined: arc. XVIII, the Moon (Fig. 90), and arc. XIX, the Sun (Fig. 91). The

90. Tarot: Arc. XVIII, *La Lune* (The Moon). Woodcut, French, 1760.

91. Tarot: Arc. XIX, *Le Soleil* (The Sun). Woodcut, French, 1760.

latter is the fiery warmth of creation, the former is an orb of strange magnetic mystery, the keeper of the tides, the bearer of creative rhythms. The sun is male, the moon female. In the Tarot, the moon is a dangerous sphere, a source of shadowy effects, an uncertain veil of intuition and magic. Its association is more with the moon-goddess Hecate, the aged crone, than with Artemis, the virginal or with Aphrodite, the ripened and complete female, Woman in the archetype. Still, the card contributes to an understanding of the hermaphroditic Devil and to the twin mystery about which Ernst said, "Of this men shall know nothing." Through the signs of this mystery deep within all creation, one ascends to the spiritual rebirth represented by arc. XX, Judgment, and to the final apotheosis of arc. XXI, the Universe.

It can be said that Ernst's suns are never wholly suns at all, but equally lunar disks. They reflect rather than radiate, and end up as sigils of the great Zero wherein the solar-lunar, male-female union is mysteriously combined. In contrast, Henri Rousseau produced a wondrous poem on the lunar theme in wholly lunar terms: *The Sleeping Gypsy* (Fig. 92). There is no way to "interpret" this work in words or ideas, for the painting truly weaves the evanescent structure of a

92. Henri Rousseau, *The Sleeping Gypsy*. Oil on canvas, 51" x 6' 7". Collection, The Museum of Modern Art, N.Y.; Gift of Mrs. Simon Guggenheim.

93. *Raja Umed Singh of Kotah Shooting Tiger*, c. 1790. Indian, Rajasthan School, from Kotah. Gouache on paper. Victoria & Albert Museum, London.

94. Henri Rousseau, *Tropical Storm, With a Tiger*, 1891. Oil on canvas. The National Gallery, London.

dream, a dream of correspondences as elusive and as real as unseen sound waves. All of which adds up to what might even be called the "fragrance" of the lunar consciousness. The eye of the lion burns as part of the constellation of stars above; its fire participates in their cold light. The gypsy is in fact an undulating radiance of light, the lion is a dream-image. They are real, yet each is imagination; each might be thought of as having dreamt the other. And the silent desert is a thought. It is the desert of psychic possibility. Rousseau could not have known the tiger-jungle-moon of Raja Umed Singh (Fig. 93), just as he undoubtedly never knew Blake's; yet his own tiger in the night (Fig. 94) draws upon the same archetypal power and so recomposes the same image in another key.

Georges Rouault inscribed the moon over Biblical towers in images that oddly parallel arc. XVIII (Fig. 95). These lunar landscapes arbitrate his mythologies of upper and lower, his saints and whores; and Rouault wrote, "I am as solitary as the lion in the desert." So did Paul Klee draw the human eye as a lunar zero in yet another jungle—of the non-self and the magical self (Fig. 96).

The case of Claude Monet is among the most remarkable. As patriarch of Impressionism—by its very nature a solar impulse—he nonetheless moved irresistibly, as the years went on, into a lunar orbit. With *Notre Dame de Rouen* (Fig. 97) he chose a directly lunar theme. For the gothic cathedrals are shrines to the Virgin (*Notre Dame*), which is the Christian parallel to the Moon Goddess. And it was an unlikely choice since works of art rarely do as the subject of works of art. In these paintings of the church at all moments of the day the light modulates, mellows, is drawn into shadow. At the end, Monet evolved those massive walls of light, *Les nymphéas* (Figs. 98a–98c)—the waterlilies—in which all luminosity deepens to a nocturnal glow. Nor is it seen directly, but is reflected in the creative medium of water—again the medium of Aphrodite, of fluid formulations, of unknown depths, of lunar quality. These fluids reflect the agitated currents of Pisces, the liquid intuition of Aquarius, the menacing dark depths of Scorpio. It is the element in which Melville's Pip saw the warp and woof of creation, and in which Schwenk

95. Georges Rouault, *Paysage animé*, 1936. Oil on canvas. Musée d'Art moderne, Paris. Photo Bulloz.

96. Paul Klee, *The moon was on the decline* . . . 1918. Gouache. Private collection. Photo Giraudon.

(overleaf)
97. Claude Monet, *Rouen Cathedral (morning)*, 1894. Oil on canvas. Jeu de Paume, Musée du Louvre, Paris.

98. a, b, c. Claude Monet, *Water Lilies*, c. 1920. Oil on canvas, triptych, 6′ 6″ x 14′. Collection, The Museum of Modern Art, N.Y.; Mrs. Simon Guggenheim Fund.

saw the living pattern of the great Zero. It is the couch of the Moon Goddess.

Earlier, having already been the victim of scandal, Edouard Manet rightly feared public reaction to his great nude, *Olympia* (Fig. 99). In this epic work, a *cause célèbre* in the birth of modern art, he had painted the goddess as a reality rather than an ideal. She was a boulevard whore, this time, of serene, disdainful flesh. She was a vision in its biological form; whereupon the predicted outcry of shock. In the halls of the Salon the official painters hung not only idealized nudes of porcelain complexion and carnal hyper-realism but scenes of rape and debauch which, in their graphic and

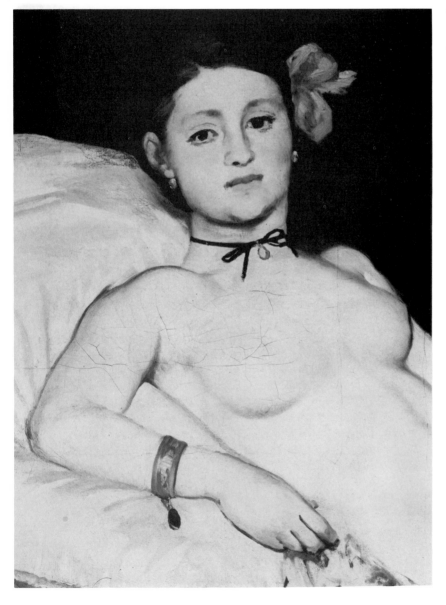

99. Edouard Manet, *Olympia*, 1865 (detail). Oil on canvas. Jeu de Paume, Musée du Louvre. Photo Bulloz.

loveless detail, are obscene even by today's standards. Yet these were not objectionable because they were not the goddess in the flesh; Manet's lady was.

It was the Goddess who turned Alfred Lord Tennyson into a weeping fool of great genius, who drove Ruskin insane for some imagined love of a minor, who hounded Swinburne into the murk of contorted passion, who presented herself to Modigliani on a loftier plane (as the equivalent of Our Lady of the cathedrals) and who sentenced the man to his death.

It would seem that any virginal young girl is the very embodiment of Artemis, and that any woman who has relinquished the bloom of her sex is the image of Hecate. But Isis, Aphrodite, Juno, Venus embody another magnitude of energy altogether. When a man is struck dumb by a woman whose beauty seems almost unreal to him, it may be that he has in effect seen the face of the goddess. It may also be that at the climax of physical passion ideal and reality interfuse, so that the goddess is again revealed. Yet, neither vision can be fixed for very long.

In his biography of the English painter Augustus John, Michael Holroyd describes the artist's fascination for the lady called Dorelia. This passage catches the Goddess theme with rare clarity:

What he desired from women was at once very simple and very difficult to achieve: it was the unknown, timelessly preserved intact: a fantasy blended with reality. Though he felt a reverence for high birth he disliked sophisticated women on the whole, and avoided women famous for their intellect and wit. Great physical beauty and fragrant simplicity were what exercised his spirit to the utmost, for behind these qualities seemed to lurk the ultimate secret, the wonder of life. Cleverness he could find elsewhere, if he needed it: he could find it in men. But in some women he could behold the inscrutable moving in step with his moods, magically deceiving tedium. For some men, stupidity mixed with a powerful dose of beauty produces this paradox, this undying spell-binding awe. For Augustus this was not so—stupid women, especially when good-looking, he had noticed, were inclined to talk too much. What he wanted was something rarer: silence. Silence was freedom. Into silence, physically eloquent, he could read everything and nothing; like Nature herself, it defied explanations, soared above them, held him entranced.[62]

John Keats had begun by addressing his Grecian urn as "Thou still unravish'd bride of quietness/Thou foster child of silence and slow time. . . ." The image of eternity expressed in perfection is parallel to John's. Timelessness, silence, the unknown, the ultimate secret, the everything and nothing: in all these the goddess and the great Zero fuse, again in Oneness.

The idea emerges today in the context of fashion. In September 1974 *Newsweek* magazine reported that Richard Avedon, the photographer, hoped to begin using more intimate or natural models in his work. *Vogue* magazine said No: " 'Using *real women* is a one shot thing,' counters Grace Mirabella. 'If the reader isn't interested in *so-and-so*, you've lost your audience. Besides *real* people are jarring. . . .' " (Italics mine.)

Paracelsus, the great seventeenth-century physician and alchemist, coined the word *alcohol*; it was born of a poetic association of the arabic *al-kohl*, fard or mascara, with the sense-stimulating effects of liquor. Indeed, both temper the factuality of physical proportions, both open the way to a magnification of vision. James Cleugh writes of the extreme methods once used in Persia to refract and prolong and intensify the act of sex in light of a supraphysical ideal. A multitude of mirrors were employed so that the lovers

would not lose sight of any aspect of the engulfing tide of eyes, lips and hair, arms and legs, breasts, stomachs and buttocks, groins and pudenda for a single second. But the tide had to come in slowly. Its motion was carefully calculated to raise the coefficient of the man's concupiscence almost imperceptibly to the point where it could balance on the very verge of ejaculation. No limit but that of utter physical exhaustion was in theory to be set to this process.[63]

However, this pursuit of an ideal made flesh, like all others, implies a vertginous point of psychic equilibrium. Cleugh says of the Persian lover:

In these aspirations he inevitably fell into the trap of sexual perversions, especially those of the *voyeur* whose ideal is the maintenance of an endless erection, since ejaculation would be found to change bliss into melancholy and regret. That climax would moreover obliterate the memory of the glorious phenomena preceding it, the gorgeous faces and figures, the splendid garments and jewels, the intoxicating motions of the dance and the thrilling resonance of music in voice or instrument. The subsequent orgasm would be exactly the same in the case of a pair of beggars as in that of a prince and princess. In both conjunctions the ceremonial element of erotic desires vanished, with everything else that distinguishes a human being from a beast.

He might well have substituted the word "magical" for "ceremonial." The great weakness of these initiatives, however, is their total dependence upon the vessel of the flesh itself within the tenuous space of time present. Once again, even given such energetic efforts of will, the incarnation of the goddess and all the power she represents is sure to be momentary. The occult connection with timelessness is incomplete; the circuit of energy-vision-consummation is inevitably broken.

The reverse, however, becomes true in the case of the Tantric magic of Asia in which pure magic, pure art, and the great sexual force are combined in unique efficacy. The fact that Tantric systems developed within both the Hindu and the Buddhist traditions, without any interchange or causal connection in their origins, is further testament to their universality as archetypal perceptions.

In these systems, sexual union assumes an integral part, as a microcosm, of the great mandala of creation. It becomes a central theme of a pattern of timelessness and energy. In the Tantric cosmology, the male force is represented as a seed which creates the female force, but the female presence, as the *yoni* or great womb, dominates creation and eventually destroys the male in the process of cosmic regeneration. During the fifteenth century, Sandro Botticelli revivified this *dénouement* in his *Venus and Mars* (Fig. 100), a painting that occupies a curious and almost comic midway point between the ancient symbolists and the Freudian ideologues. In our own time, Paul Delvaux has depicted the male quite literally "beside himself" in the power of the moon and the goddess (Fig. 101).

The Tantric vision is consummated on four levels *which are in fact one*. The *yantra* is the tangible symbolic presence

100. Sandro Botticelli, *Venus and Mars*, 15th C. Oil on wood. The National Gallery, London.

101. Paul Delvaux, *l'Adieu*, 1964. Oil on canvas. Stooshnoff Gallery, London.

of the great force in icon or mandala. The *mantra* is the intoned syllabic chant of the great rhythm in audible form. A third level is the anthropoid presence of the force in the form of the Goddess herself. A fourth—or first—is the actual act of sex, ritually inscribed upon the cosmic and timeless map.

Philip Rawson speaks of

. . . an image of the Goddess, in wood, stone, metal or dough, which represents her as a beautiful girl who, as she dances crazy with love, lets down her hair, spreading out the worlds, and binds it up again, bringing them to their end. The Tantrika's mind is continually absorbed in that shining and fascinating image. Every woman appears to him clothed in it. But it is not, for him, the woman who personifies the Goddess, but the Goddess who appears in the woman. The charm of the inner image is for him far greater than that of any actual woman; and the justification for every art-made icon of the Goddess used in Tantric worship is that it promotes the intensity of that inner image, while at the same time it can never imprison the mind within its own merely material forms." [64]

In other words, here is at once a cosmology and an actual system in which the enigma that tormented Augustus John and laid Tennyson low can begin to be resolved. Rawson makes a point about the underlying beliefs of Tantrism which at this juncture will sound not unfamiliar to the reader:

Tantra holds that our impression that things exist outside ourselves is really the result of an encounter between fields of energy. A rainbow only appears when sunrays, atmospheric processes and the optical activity of an observer come together in a certain relationship in space and time. In Tantra's understanding all other objects, no matter how dense they may seem, like rocks, plants and men, are so intimately interwoven with men's ideas as to be inseparable. They result in the same way from the collision and collusion of forces. And such forces can only be defined in terms of time; they are sub-functions of the processes of time. [65]

So Rutherford, so Einstein, so Planck, so Eddington; it took science fourteen centuries of analytical method to match this synthesis of occult vision. When Crowley said that magic is science in the flesh he knew whereof he spoke. Inevitably, one returns to the great underlying flux of energy itself. It may be useful to take notice of the original nature of the god Eros:

Among Aphrodite's normal companions the most important was Eros. Unknown in Homeric times, he appears in Hesiod's *Theogony* as the son of Erubus and the Night. His role was to co-ordinate the elements which constitute the universe. It is he who "brings harmony to chaos" and permits life to develop. This primitive deity, a semi-abstract personification of cosmic force, has little resemblance to the traditional Eros whose physiognomy was only developed in later times. [66]

The earlier deity is in fact the very opposite of the later; not the eroticism of limitless desire and resulting disproportion, but rather an almost Tantric-like image of cosmic balance. Hesiod's Eros married Psyche, whose name is the Greek word for soul. It was said that Psyche's beauty was such that even Aphrodite was jealous of her.

Lucas Cranach portrayed *Cupid Complaining to Venus* (Fig. 102); the infant god is tormented by bees which seem not to affect his beautiful and serene mother. And Bronzino went further. His *Allegory of Lust* (Fig. 103) might easily be called an allegory of delusion. There Cupid is actually seduced by the Moon Goddess, his own mother. They are sur-

102. Lucas Cranach, *Cupid Complaining to Venus*, 16th C. Oil on wood. The National Gallery, London.

103. Bronzino, *Allegory of Lust*, 16th C. Oil panel. The National Gallery, London.

103. Bronzino, *Allegory of Lust*, 16th C. Oil panel. The National Gallery, London.

rounded by the figures of jealousy, lust, deception, and the masks of illusion.

The sixteenth-century painters of the Court of Fontainebleau under François I were able to find a singularly graceful solution to the problem of blending the eternal archetype with the fleeting reality. This young and robust monarchy which had risen from a venerable, gothic past was able to produce a unique coincidence of the fleshly and the formal. Gabrielle d'Estrées clasps her sister's nipple in a tableau as austere as a gothic frieze and as intimate as a vignette of the Belle Epoque (Fig. 104). The ladies of the bath (Fig. 105) bring

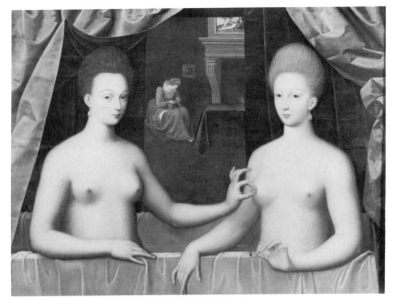

104. Ecole de Fontainebleau, *Gabrielle d'Estrees and one of her sisters*, 16th C. Oil on canvas. Musée du Louvre, Paris. Photo Giraudon.

105. Ecole de Fontainebleau, *Scene de bain*, 16th C. Private collection. Photo Bulloz, Paris.

106. Ecole de Fontainebleau, *Diane de Poitiers*, 16th C. Oil on canvas. Private collection. Photo Bulloz, Paris.

107. *Eve tempted*, 12th–13th C. Autun Cathedral.

108. Félicien Rops, *The Diabolic Ones*, 1882. Heliogravure and etching. Private collection.

109. Max Klinger, *The Bear and the Elf*, 1878–80. Etching. Photo Bulloz.

archaic Rome into Renaissance Paris; Diane de Poitiers in her vaporously cloaked nudity is at once porcelain and flesh, a fact and an idea (Fig. 106).

Poets have dealt with this enigma of the intersection of goddess and woman in countless forms. The medieval sculptors of Autun (Fig. 107) showed Eve tempted by the diabolical serpent (whose coil can be said to parallel the horns of Behemoth). Centuries later, Félicien Rops depicted the same forces united in an orgy of mutual sacrifice (Fig. 108). For Max Klinger (Fig. 109) the drama takes the shape of a surreal animal confrontation. And Paul Delvaux unfolds an epic panorama (Fig. 110) in which the female presence seen as goddess and as human, nude and clothed, confronts ineluctable death amid a lunar labyrinth and a lunar wilderness.

110. Paul Delvaux, *Venus Asleep*, 1944. Oil on canvas. The Tate Gallery, London.

The duality posed is one of form, of matter, of the Devil of the Tarot, of those material wonders which reflect creation and embody energy, but which at the same time limit and obscure the pure light. Shelley voiced the despair of the romantic poet before this light when he wrote *Adonais*, his elegy on the death of John Keats:

> The One remains, the many change and pass;
> Heaven's light forever shines, Earth's shadows fly;
> Life, like a dome of many-coloured glass,
> Stains the white radiance of Eternity,
> Until Death tramples it to fragments—Die,
> If thou wouldst be with that which thou dost seek!
> Follow where all is fled!—Rome's azure sky,
> Flowers, ruins, statues, music, words, are weak,
> The glory they transfuse with fitting truth to speak.[67]

So had Keats himself bridled under the limitations of the mortal coil:

My spirit is too weak—mortality
  Weighs heavily on me like unwilling sleep,
  And each imagin'd pinnacle and steep
Of godlike hardship, tells me I must die
Like a sick eagle looking at the sky.
  Yet 'tis a gentle luxury to weep
  That I have not the cloudy winds to keep,
Fresh for the opening of the morning's eye.
Such dim-conceived glories of the brain
  Bring round the heart an indescribable feud;
So do these wonders a most dizzy pain,
  That mingles Grecian grandeurs with the rude
Wasting of old Time—with a billowy main—
  A sun—a shadow of a magnitude.[68]

The Saint and the City

The romantic eye is attuned to distance. It views the shadow of a magnitude through extremes of vast possibility and ultimate destruction. There is a quality to it akin to adolescence; and it might be said that if the Moon Goddess governs all art, it is Artemis the virgin who directs the romantic impulse. Romanticism is a preorgasmic art; like those Persian idealists of the flesh it seeks to prolong the life of the imagination, the light of ecstasy, and to deny the zone of anticlimax. At the other extreme, realism denies the imagination, presents life in the cold light of perceptual fact and accountable events. This is the region of Hecate, the crone. So that it can even be said that realism and art are contradictory values. A painter may be "naturalistic"; but imagination creates reality, determines the shape of energy. Hence art as the medium of occult perception—the point at which the word "reality" begins to assume real meaning—answers to the brilliant and complex light of Aphrodite. Art's emergence is symbolized by the divine marriage of Eros and Psyche.

In two remarkable books, *The Man Who Died* by D. H. Lawrence and *Siddhartha* by Hermann Hesse, this issue of order and ecstasy, form and passion, arises. Lawrence retells and transfigures the story of Christ resurrected; Hesse reworks the story of the Buddha's assumption. In each case, a total commitment to a divine spirit beyond the forms of the world is revised so as to take in the sensual rhythms of creation. The Christ reborn sees that he had asked the impossible of men; he sees that spirit dwells live in the flesh. He sees the beauty of Isis; he learns the magic of the Goddess. In the same way Siddhartha learns the totality of an energy in which the world and eternity are one. He lives the life of an ascetic, then of materialism and of carnal desires, and then of despairing perplexity. At last, a new vision emerges. It should not now surprise the reader to find that Hesse portrays the great teacher as a river:

He looked lovingly into the flowing water, into the transparent green, into the crystal lines of its wonderful design. He saw bright pearls rise from the depths, bubbles swimming on the mirror, sky-blue reflected in them. The river looked at him with a thousand eyes—green, white, crystal, sky-blue. . . . He saw that the water continually flowed and flowed and yet it was always there; it was always the same and yet every moment it was new. Who could understand, conceive this? He did not understand it; he was only aware of a dim suspicion, a faint memory, divine voices.

The lessons of the silent teacher deepen and expand. The great Oneness becomes an omnipresent reality:

This stone is stone; it is also animal, God and Buddha. I do not respect and love it because it was one thing and will become something else, but because it had already long been everything and always in everything. I love it just because it is a stone. . . . I see value and meaning in each of its fine markings and cavities, in the yellow, in the grey, in the hardness and the sound of it when I knock it, in the dryness or dampness of its surface. There are stones that feel like oil or soap, that look like leaves or sand, and each one is different and worships Om in its own way; each one is Brahman. At the same time it is very much stone, oily or soapy, and that is just what pleases me and seems wonderful and worthy of worship. But I will say no more about it. Words do not express thoughts very well. They always become a little different immediately they are expressed, a little distorted, a little foolish. And yet it also pleases me and seems right that what is of value and wisdom to one man seems nonsense to another.[69]

The cosmic egg of Tantra is perhaps the most potent expression of that real but symbolic stone which vibrates with life. Like Blake's flower expressing infinity, it is a particle and a totality, a detail and a cosmology. The eloquence of its expression is englobed in its silence. It too is a mandala, a labyrinthine voice in the desert. When expressed as the fertilized world-egg composed of the precincts and forces of energy (Fig. 111), it bears immediate association with the Tantric conception of the universe as a cosmic river of time and reality (Fig. 112). We are back, inevitably, to the helix and the circle. One can now begin to view the potency of the precinct with added respect. It does not simply protect, it also invokes; if it is there for the exclusion of outside forces it is also there, like the labyrinth of nerves and synapses within the body, for a union with omnipresent energies. It is a kind of filter. This is true not only of the ritual sand paintings of the Navahos but also of the actual walls and chambers of man's own precinct, the City.

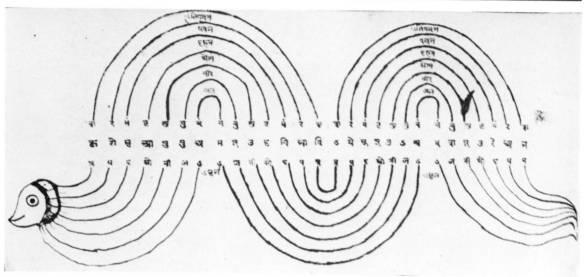

111. *Fertilized World-Egg Composed of the Precincts and Forces of Energy.* Tantric, Rajasthan, 18th C. Gouache on paper. Photo Thames & Hudson Ltd., London.

112. *The Eternal Recurrence of the Seven-Fold Divisions of the Universe as a Cosmic River of Time and Reality.* Rajasthan, 19th C. Jaina manuscript; ink on paper. Photo Thames & Hudson, Ltd., London.

The City is man's physical response to the desert. Its angles represent the furthest point in his evolution from the fluid waters out of which he crawled in prototype millions of years ago. The chamber is more than a physical place; it encloses an atmosphere, a mystery, a domain of vibrations. The building itself is more than an outer shell; it also bespeaks an inner architecture that mirrors the men who chose to create it. The Greeks and Romans were sensitive to this portion of the spirit. So were the painters of the Italian Renaissance whose work was born of a renascence of Classical values. In our own century, after Monet drew a lunar light over the lunar presence of Rouen cathedral, the cubists and the surrealists pursued the theme with renewed reverence.

During the fifteenth century, Carlo Crivelli painted a work in which an anthology of occult symbolism centers about a confrontation of void and labyrinth within the precinct of the city of Ancona: *The Annunciation with Saint Emidius* (Fig. 113). The panel is an extraordinary case in point, for it encompasses so many of the key points discussed thus far. It appears as a nexus of occult precepts.

The city, defined in minute, idealized detail, becomes a field of classic proportion, a grid of verticals and horizontals upon which the oblique shaft of the miracle—as light—takes place. Emidius, patron saint of the town, holds its replica (detail, Fig. 114). Is this facsimile a model of the actual city, or is the city a concrete model of the spiritual ideal?

The angular presence of the whole contrasts—and participates—with the great wheel of celestial light (Fig. 115) whose beam penetrates, through the microwheel of light surrounding the bird of the Holy Ghost, to the Virgin. The diadem on the Virgin's brow is yet another circle, akin to that found on the brow of the Buddhas of India and China. The halo, symbol of holiness, recapitulates the theme.

The angel is an androgynous figure which recalls not Behemoth but the dual male-female, solar-lunar nature of all creation. The sinuous, rhythmical flow of its wings and robes (Fig. 116) responds to the fluidity of forms yearning for the great circle, with which we began.

The city is peopled by thirteen mortal figures of whom two alone take notice of the miracle while the others circulate in the temporal sphere. The man under the arch looks with apparent curiosity at what appears to be a strange ray of light; he seems to be puzzled. Only the little girl at left gazes with undivided fascination at the phenomenon. Hers is the vision of a child, still capable of direct perception unabridged by association, induction, syllogism, rationalism. For her the angel's wings might have been seen immediately as magical, rhythmic presences—even when seen right-side up. She is by nature closer to the mystical, the hallucinatory, the occult.

Furthermore, the aegis of the miracle is light—a power of light. So it is that Crivelli casts his scene in a hallucinatory superbrilliance, hyper-reality, akin to that described by Huxley. The lines of perspective may conform to optical "realities" of the humanistic Renaissance—but with a real difference which is found in many other works of the period as well. Crivelli maintains an absolute sharpness of focus ranging from the heavens to the near foreground. For the human eye this is an optical impossibility; for the inner eye as optic of the Imagination according to Blake's vision, it is a revelation.

The intersection of occult themes becomes particularly graphic here. However, we have run across any number of such overlappings. The labyrinth, the desert, the solar and lunar presences, the ubiquitous fluidity of form as archetype, the intersection of one brand of magic and another, interlink as in a musical fugue. For as soon as the eye succeeds in penetrating occult depths—the world of primal energies, even if seen in refraction—it begins to exert a perceptive power that might be likened to a magnetic field. Symbols, clues, meanings, correspondences, images, forms, colors will arise to that power much as iron filings pattern themselves about the poles of a magnet. The artist and magician alike know this harmonic current with a visceral awareness, a function of will. One might postulate a law: If a work of art is genuinely occult in at least one sense, it is likely to be so in other directions as well.

Technique follows perception, but often it follows with mysterious grace. Early in the fifteenth century, Antonello da Messina arrived in Venice with the secrets of the technique of oil painting. Previously, the Italians had worked in fresco, or in any case, with flat or matte pigments. But Antonello had come into contact with Flemish painting, the glowing brilliance of Van Eyck, conjured in oil pigments. In all likelihood he had actually traveled to the Lowlands. Through this contact a new magic was born. The intense symbolism of Byzantine art with its golden sky and formal rectitude was

(overleaf)
113. Carlo Crivelli, *The Annunciation with St. Emidius*, 1486. Panel, transferred to canvas, painted surface. The National Gallery, London.

114. Detail of Pl. 113.

115. Detail of Pl. 113.

116. Detail of Pl. 113 (reproduced upside-down).

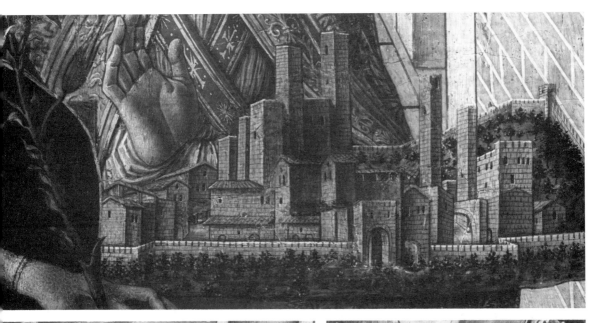

gone. Human properties had been substituted for the reflection of godly ones. But now, by a mysterious marriage of Flemish coolness and Italian warmth, the means to another hyper-reality were reconstituted. The waters of the Lowland and Venetian canals were conjoined in a crucible of light. A newly hallucinatory image beyond the current norms of perception became possible. That good and generous man of influential genius, Giovanni Bellini, did not hesitate to maximize the possibility by transforming his own work; and no seer proved more capable in that direction than Bellini's own brother-in-law, Andrea Mantegna, who loved to blend the labyrinth and the desert, and heaven and earth, in hallucinatory detail.

Five centuries later, through another function of will, the young Spaniard Pablo Picasso came to Paris and saw a direct, noncausal connection between the luminous geometry of Paul Cézanne, the ancient purities of Iberian sculpture, and the totemic austerities of African sculpture. Of this the movement called Cubism was born. It was again an art of the City, of angles, of inner architectures. Picasso and Georges Braque exploded the perimeters of form, and even broke down the human body, to reconstitute matter in the power of another light. They did not know that at the same time Rutherford, Einstein, and Planck were reinvestigating molecules in the same way. They took Cézanne's planes and volumes, Seurat's shimmering megaliths of light, African rhythms, and redefined the world.

Nor must one omit the fact that at the same time Henri "le douanier" Rousseau was in their midst—this little man who played the fiddle in public gardens in order to live, who was justly if naively accused of "innocence," who dislodged Blake's tiger from the zoo, who placed the glowing sigil of the moon over a new Imagination, who brought the desert-jungle into Paris through wholly psychic means. The mandolin beside the Sleeping Gypsy was not yet the cubist guitar, but the music had already largely been scored. The key to it all might very well be called music, in the same way that Don Juan admonished Casteneda to stop trying to look at the world and begin hearing it.

How is music made—even in the usual sense? One man,

using only mind, puts ink to paper on a lined score that produces no sound at all; nothing physical has happened yet. Then another man draws a bow across the stretched length of a cat's intestines while another blows through a wooden tube, his colleague into a brass vessel, and another beats against a tightened length of some other animal's skin. While many such men work together in a sort of cult or coven (for the "score" produced by the first man is a hermetic document legible only to certain initiates), still another adept, who seems to have some power over the others, waves his arms about according to sensate ritual and somehow coordinates their actions. Since the result is Handel's *Messiah* or Mozart's *Jupiter*, the whole process is dismissed as an exquisite sensation, one that is entirely normal, answering to the laws of physics and of neurology. Perhaps it is. Yet it must be admitted that the whole of this behavior serves to express, through a weird physical process, a psychic certainty that began with Handel or Mozart as pure mind. Music critics often are moved to comment that the physical performance is an approximate shadow of the invisible reality.

So it was that the cubists evoked inner chords of light, occult equations, inner harmonies. By 1909, Braque was already painting La Roche-Guyon as a city of light (Fig. 117), as occult a presence as Greco's Toledo, a city drawn upward, in a twisting flame of motion (Fig. 118). During the next two years the process deepens, the equation purifies: the nude, the city, and the guitar are drawn into Oneness, the unity of crackling, vibrating light-energy. Art history, in time, calls all this Analytical Cubism. But it is far more. As timelessness it is far more a synthesis of magic. Cocteau again hit the mark when he wrote, "A holy family is not necessarily a holy family; it may also consist of a pipe, a pint of beer, a pack of cards, and a pouch of tobacco." [70]

By 1912, the period called synthetic cubism began with the invention of collage. Bits of wallpaper, fabric, newspaper, fragments of musical scores were made to participate in what Picasso insisted was not *trompe l'oeil* but *trompe l'esprit*. Shadows became realities, substances became pure space, particles of form were held in orbit by perceptual energy. It all encapsulated—yet no more so than in the "analytical" phase—

117. Georges Braque, *View of La Roche-Guyon*, 1909. Oil on canvas. Stedelijk van Abbe Museum, Eindhoven. Photo Thames & Hudson Ltd., London.

118. El Greco, *View of Toledo*, 1609. Oil on canvas. The Metropolitan Museum of Art, Bequest of Mrs. H. O. Havemeyer, 1929. The H. O. Havemeyer Collection.

the sense of Rutherford's atom and the astonishing equilibrium of a subatomic universe of ever turbulent energy.

Inevitably, the perceptual currents initiated by Picasso and Braque sparked other visions. As early as 1909–1910, Fernand Léger painted his *Nudes in the Forest* (Fig. 119). At the same time Gino Severini, a spokesman of futurism, produced *Pan-Pan à Monico* (Fig. 120). Both broke physical masses down into psi fields of energy. There is no space here to tell the full story of this impulse during these years. However, the sense of it is manifest. Marcel Duchamp interfused space and time in his *Nude Descending a Staircase* (Fig. 121), and the Italian futurists took up that theme with obsessive ardor. Their leader, Umberto Boccioni, saw the human figure turned spectral with sheer energy, under such titles as *Muscular Dynamism* (Fig. 122) and *Unique Forms of Continuity in Space*.

Just as none of these men was aware of the respective tide in physical science, so were they unaware of the occult revival engaged in by the Order of the Golden Dawn or the experiments in will undertaken by Crowley. Yet all three —cubism, atomic science, and occult experimentation—were strangely parallel workings of the league of vision, and all three were of the nature of secret societies whose language had to be phrased in hermetic symbols accessible only to the initiate. Not a dozen men of science could claim to grasp Einstein's thought in its entirety. Of the cubists and their allies, Picasso and Braque were the last of the original group to exhibit works born of exploration rather than expression, and which were not there for admiration but for revelation. Of those who composed the O.T.O. and the Golden Dawn, none was apparently able to match Crowley's vivification of mystical processes through the medium of psychic will. Crowley wrote of magic as the power of the mind to change nature. So Einstein and Picasso; we began with the observation that man is process, not reality, and that vision is what shapes the world; so Blake, so Castaneda. The great challenge is precisely the manifestation of that vision through will. This is the promise of the occult future. And the reason for hope that a deepening and an expansion of such vision is possible lies precisely in the loveless, nonsensual levi-

119. Fernand Léger, *Nudes in the Forest*, 1909–10. Oil on canvas. Rijksmuseum Kröller-Müller, Otterlo.

120. Gino Severini, *Pan-Pan à Monico* (copy), original of 1909–11 destroyed. Oil on canvas. Musée National d'Art Moderne, Paris.

121. Marcel Duchamp, *Nude Descending a Staircase, No. 2*, 1912. Oil on canvas. Philadelphia Museum of Art.

NU DESCENDANT UN ESCALIER

133

122. Umberto Boccioni, *Muscular Dynamism*, 1913. Charcoal on paper, 34″ x 23¼″. Collection, The Museum of Modern Art, N.Y.; Purchase.

athan of a world that will increasingly force the mind—psyche and soma—inward. The deprivation of the outer eye will demand a new acclimation of the inner eye.

Some degree of this power of concentration or this singularity of psychic light is also what wins the dancer, the acrobat, the torero, the athlete a triumph over physical limitations often described as magical in another dimension. The dancer performs a ritual in which physical grace opposes the force of gravity. The trapeze artist balanced on a cable stakes his life upon that opposition, just as the torero before his bull gambles upon an inner certainty, a harmony of grace and will, which, like Blake's flower or the halo of Crivelli's Virgin, can be said to implicate the entire universe. At such points as these there is no safety barrier between will and death.

The faculty, this intensity in which the self and non-self meet in the light of certain underlying energies, remains to be cultivated. What the bullfighter experiences in the arena, and the acrobat under the ray of a spotlight, the poet confronts in a terrible solitude of apparent free will and uncertain dimensions. Cocteau has quoted the only surviving reminiscence of El Greco the man. It deserves repeating:

I went yesterday to El Greco's house in order to take a walk with him in the town. The weather was very fine with delightful spring sunshine which made everyone happy. The town seemed to be *en fête*. I was astonished on entering El Greco's studio to find the curtains drawn so tightly that one could hardly see anything. El Greco was sitting on a chair neither working nor sleeping.
He did not want to come out with me, for the daylight disturbed his inner light.[71]

"Neither working nor sleeping"; was this meditation? It was in any case a point of focus in which the inner eye finds a certain wavelength, a certain clarity, just as the laser beam must be adjusted to its brutal or intricately delicate power. The outer light had to be dimmed to near blackness as a velvet curtain might be used to set off the pale luminosity of a precious gem or to expose the white, blue, red, and yellow color-heat architecture of a flame.

In this way the mystic, the poet, the magician attune their mechanisms to other worlds, worlds within. In 1947, the American, Russian-born painter Maurice Sievan—a mystic by inclination rather than by doctrine—painted a work called *Evanescence* (Fig. 123). Its gradations of light and form become a map of the physical, etheric, and astral planes. Light is the key connection in every sense. Fifteen years later, he completed the painting called *Buxtabutz* (Fig. 124), in

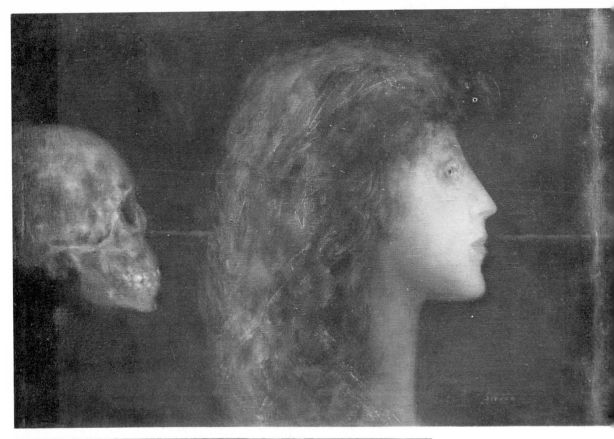

123. Maurice Sievan, *Evanescence*, 1947. Oil on canvas. Collection Mr. and Mrs. Maurice Vanderwoude. Photo O. E. Nelson.

124. Maurice Sievan, *Buxtabutz*, 1962. Oil on canvas.

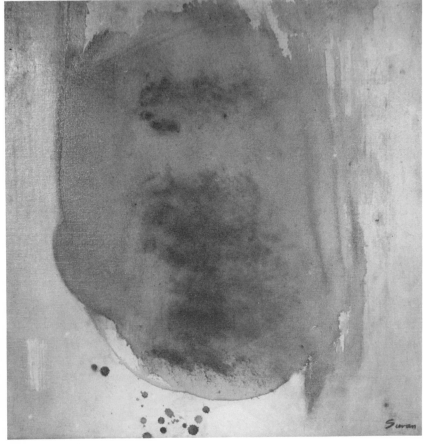

which the physical has been subsumed into the sovereignty of light. The uninitiate may see these two works as "a complete change of style." In fact, their continuity is manifest. As equations of light-energy they are almost the same work. And the fact that the later painting is astonishingly close to images conjured up by Victor Hugo a century earlier—images Sievan had never seen—testifies to the originality of both men's visions of an archetypal source.

This process of seeing with the mind's eye implies a simultaneous tuning of the outer and the inner light. During one of the worst London fogs of the last century the blind were employed as guides for the seeing. There was no visibility, and the blind alone were able to navigate in space. Alter atmospheric conditions sufficiently and the priorities of vision end up reversed. The unbeliever—as opposed to the true skeptic—is told of a ghost, recoils superstitiously from the "specter" of balance-threatening creative possibility, and snaps out, "It must have been a trick of the light!" What then are X-ray photographs? What is the power of the laser? What is a self-portrait by Rembrandt? What are the tender solidity of Chardin's plums and the transparent flesh of a Pascin nude? Why is the lovelight in Miranda's eyes something more than a mere trait? Why are bistros candle-lit, and discothèques psychedelic? What was the Venus seen by Proust on awakening, and what was the resplendent dawn seen by Blake alone as a chorus of angels singing for joy? All of them were in one way or another "a trick of the light"; the German word for art is *kunst* which also happens to mean *trick* (Fig. 125).

Such modulations of vision range from super-sanity to madness; but since that particular spectrum is circular the two meet at a certain point, a point sometimes difficult to distinguish and sometimes embodying both qualities. This fact was brought home to André Breton, "high priest of Surrealism," in the person of that quirk of nature and antinature, the girl called Nadja. That apparent chance brought this beam of intense and eccentric light into the path of surrealism's chief theoretician is one of those startling "coincidences" in the psi swarm which are themselves a factor in the great equation.

125. Toyen, *Legend of the Light*, 1946. Oil on canvas. Private collection, Paris.

Who was Nadja? Apparently a presence, in fact a girl encountered in Paris on the rue de Lafayette by grace of her hallucinatory eyes, and in the end of a kind of magnetic field of psychic force. When Breton asks her who she is; she replies, "I am the soul-errant."

They agree to meet at certain appointed cafés; when Nadja fails to arrive they nonetheless meet elsewhere—by chance. Breton kisses her; she repeats, twice, "The communion takes place in silence." Then she explains that the kiss leaves her an impression of something sacred, "where her teeth took the place of the Host." On the following day Breton receives a postcard from Louis Aragon in Italy: it bears a detail from Uccello's *The Profanation of the Host*. Incessantly, Nadja's words are the source of coincidence; they bear direct allusion to something Breton has just read or written, references the girl could not possibly have known about. Beyond this, her words trace a poetic labyrinth in which Breton himself finds it difficult, vertiginous, to follow. She inhabits her own world whose frontiers surface momentarily in symbolic sketches and phrases: "The lion's claw embraces the breast of the vine." They dine on the terrace of a restaurant in the Place Dauphine. Nadja indicates a window opposite: "Do you see that window, over there? It's dark, like all the others. In a minute it will light up. It will be red." In a minute the window is suddenly lit, and the light filters through a red curtain. Breton is unnerved. The waiter appears almost hypnotized by Nadja's presence. He acts clumsily, and in the end breaks several glasses. In all, Breton grows increasingly fearful, and at last finds it best to part with Nadja. Later she disappears into the arcane privacy of her inner world, and is incarcerated.

Maurice Nadeau, in *The History of Surrealism*, is moved to comment:

It is a slight story, but bears an enormous weight. It constitutes an entry into the lives of beings who are beyond life; it is the eruption of ghosts who quite naturally hold out their hands to the living. Madness? The word is easily said. And what is madness? What difference does madness make in the facts reported? How does it explain the countless coincidences and the true prediction of events which depend on neither of the partners? Did

Nadja go mad as soon as she was confined? Was she mad before? Did Breton, as some have said, cause a deterioration of her state? What matter! Beyond appearances, Nadja is a being who lives henceforth in us, with us.[72]

Nadeau's "What matter!" might be taken as a fairly cavalier reaction, for it may be that Nadja's twilight lucidity later turned into a stygian hell. Yet while that light flickered she was of the family of Melville's Pip, and even of Coleridge or De Quincey in hallucinogenic trance. When writing *Nadja*, Breton for the moment drops the voice of the rhetorical leader and speaks in a sometimes tremulous hush. How odd that fate or chance or whatever one chooses to call the cause presented this man with the living incarnation of that dream consciousness, that "paranoia," which he demanded of painters and poets. And how ironical it is that Breton should have blanched and fled when confronted with the undiluted fulfillment of his hopes. Of course, what daunted him was not the unreal or surreal Nadja, the hallucinatory speech or the magical vision, or even the sphynxian factor of prophecy, but precisely their mortal shell, the person, the girl, which lent these powers gigantic proportion and grotesque relief. It was the fleshly reality that touched this psychic landscape with a glow of horror, and which tempered Breton's speech to a whisper, and sent him fleeing back to the sturdier timbers of talent and genius. He had skirted the abyss, and that was quite enough.

So that the life and death of vision, the antipodes of illumination and madness, coil and evolve, with the same irresistible motion of water seeking the perfect sphere, towards another great circle. Odd that at this very moment in time science is also moving closer and closer to its own postulation of Oneness in terms of energy—while simultaneously running into ever more troubling complexities in its effort to make sense of the energies within the atom. There is a kind of double drama here, a conflict which science finds more difficult to resolve than do either magic or art.

On November 2, 1973, *The New York Times* reported a story by Walter Sullivan to the effect that physics had suddenly found new, though debated, support for the "Unified Field Theory":

As a result of experiments conducted in Switzerland, some physicists have come to believe that two of the basic forms of nature —electromagnetism and the less well known "weak" force of radioactive decay—may be expressions of the same phenomenon. . . . This would support the long sought goal of a "unified field theory" relating the four seemingly diverse processes in physics, chemistry and biology.

The entire proposition again implies the primacy of energy. It also has to be seen in the context of some forty years of research by Dr. Harold S. Burr of Yale, Dr. Wilder Penfield, and others, leading to the conclusion that ". . . thought is independent of the physical brain and is another kind of field —a 'thought-field.' " [73] The hypothesis is that "fields of Life" called L-fields, which can be measured with voltmeters, are in fact electromagnetic fields which "mould the ever-changing material of the cells." Dr. Burr comments,

These fields regulate and control all living things. Though infinitely complicated, like other electromagnetic fields they are influenced by the greater fields of the Universe. So man is an integral part of the Universe and shares its purpose and its destiny.

This is Blake again, and to perfection! The implications of this theory are immense. They begin to suggest a scientific basis for the claims of astrology; far more important, they begin to chart some possible codification of the principles behind our vague and mysterious psi field, in which extrasensory perception, clairvoyance, prophecy, astral projection, and the active zone of magical will, take place. A new light has been cast upon the wonder of the great Oneness.

In the meantime, the physicists in their laboratories have penetrated ever deeper into subreal labyrinths of the atom. From those depths they send up messages of revelation, and also of perplexity. Not many years ago, it was taught that the atom consisted of only three particles: a nucleus of positive protons and neutral neutrons surrounded by negative electrons in orbit. Science swore by it. Today, *over one hundred* subatomic particles have been seen or tracked or postulated, including muons, pirons, hadrons, leptons, and kaons, some of which may result from the decomposition of photons; others, like positrons, from the mere collision of still other particles. And the maze extends further. "To hunt the quark" was at first a phrase meaning to seek the existence of the ultimate particle. Today, however, the new theoretical model of the atom hypothesizes blue, white, and red quarks, and even, yes, the "charm" quark. *Strangeness* is now the technical term for a factor discussed in the physical laboratory. Furthermore, as of the fall of 1974, the behavior of all the mysterious subatomic entities continues to surprise and bewilder the experts tunneling below.

Most recently, in March, 1975, Dr. Werner Heisenberg published an article that went all the way and broached the possibility of an end to classical science as it has been known since Copernicus: "What is really needed is a change in fundamental concepts. We will have to abandon the philosophy of Democritus and the concept of fundamental elementary particles. And, instead, we will have to accept the concept of fundamental symmetries which is a concept out of the philosophy of Plato." [74]

The most important Neoplatonist of modern times, as Kathleen Raine has pointed out, was William Blake. And what Dr. Heisenberg's words imply is precisely that mind, not matter, is the great key. Whereupon the whole of ancient gnosis and Neoplatonist thought will have to be reexamined as testimony rather than as antiquity.

One imagines William Blake chuckling with wry amusement; and the Buddha—he who had either "solved" the mystery of the river or had become as one with it—smiling that perfection of a smile, with just a touch of mockery. One likes to remember that Voltaire, the heavyweight champion of arrogant rationalism, spent his old age with a priest at his side, and that Henri Poincaré, as Cocteau testifies, knew better all along.

The gates of the infinite are open as never before in the modern world. The problem is again one of *seeing* and of *will*. There exists a capacity of the mind which Colin Wilson has termed Faculty X, a faculty of concentration or illumination that permits the mind to leap beyond induction and deduction to a magnified sense of reality to grasp things *whole*. This is what sparks the eye of the magician and establishes art over science.

Earlier in this century an odd concatenation occurred in these spheres when the Russian-born Wassily Kandinsky and the Dutch master Piet Mondrian came into contact with the Theosophist thought of Madame Blavatsky and the spiritualist Thought-Forms of Annie Besant and C. W. Leadbeater. It was a most unlikely confluence of minds.

Shortly before her death, Helena Petrovna Blavatsky was still able to tell Yeats, "I write, write, write, as the Wandering Jew walks, walks, walks." [75] She knew an irrepressible life force; even with youth long behind her—and at 232 pounds—she retained a mysterious feminine allure. In perpetual dynamic activity her life parallels that of Crowley. In Colin Wilson's words:

She . . . travelled, according to her own account, in Mexico, Texas, India, Canada and Tibet—the last was almost impossible for a woman to enter, and she was turned back twice. [A] circus job seems to have ruined her sex life; she fell off a horse and displaced her womb—which, a doctor certified later, made abstention unavoidable; she later declared, "I am lacking something, and the place is filled up with some crooked cucumber." Returning to Italy from Greece in her fortieth year, the *Eumonia* blew up, and only seventeen of its four hundred passengers survived; she described limbs and heads falling about her as she swam. [76]

There is enough even in this one tragicomic passage to suggest the causes of a well-deserved "nervous breakdown," but nothing of the sort happened. In a mystic of her dimensions the self often appears as a mere incidental companion to the power of mind. Blavatsky went on. What she went on to is a matter of debate to this day. Verbose, profane, reverent, erudite, implacable, she believed herself to be the chosen medium for the Ancient Wisdom of two Masters then incarnated as Indians in the Himalayas. One, she said, had previously been Pythagoras. On the other hand, her Theosophical Society—which still very much exists—was prompted by her interest in the dimensions of the Egyptian pyramids whose "laws of proportion" appeared to be the key to active magic. Since her time, artists, archaeologists, mathematicians, architects, and now physicists, have come to explore the same questions.

Henri Michaux etches a vibrating, shimmering pyramid

that is more a pulsation of the psi idea than a structure (Fig. 126). Damian constructs an austere step-pyramid in homage to the mysterious psychic dignity such a monument itself appears to radiate (Fig. 127). Their points of view, like Blavatsky's, begin with an intuitive or visceral response to proportion.

On December 6, 1974, David Michelmore reported for the AP that ". . . Chefren's giant pyramid at Giza has turned back man's most sophisticated attempt to find the pharoah's burial chamber." The pyramid proved immune to penetration by radar waves: "The scientists found that the radar signals, transmitted by a 30,000 volt 'sounder', disappeared after traveling only a few feet because of the unexpectedly high moisture content in the pyramid. . . ." [77]

That moisture, while mysterious, had been noted many years ago by the French investigator Bovis who explored the adjoining pyramid of Cheops, Chefren's father. Bovis found

126. Henri Michaux, *Etching*, 1963. Le Point Cardinal. Photo Jean Dubout.

127. Damian, *Pyramid Staircase: Blue Black*, 1965. Relief. Galerie Stadler, Paris. Photo Augustin Dumage.

that the bodies of dead cats had mummified naturally within the tomb. And he was able to verify that the same occurs if a dead cat is placed within any scale-model pyramid *of the same proportion and same north-south-east-west axis*. We are back to Don Juan's desert here, within a labyrinth of classic power.

Each investigation only adds further mystery. The AP dispatch did not mention that the same team composed of scientists from the American Research Center and Ein Shams University had discovered five years before that the pyramid somehow seemed to scramble or confuse all cosmic-ray patterns in a concerted X-ray attempt. Lyall Watson, in *Supernature*, quotes the project leader: "This is scientifically impossible. Call it what you will—occultism, the curse of the pharaohs, sorcery, or magic, there is some force that defies the laws of science at work in the pyramid." [78]

The occult propositions are surely the most elegant proposals. Cirlot gives Marc Saunier's view on this:

He regards the pyramid as a synthesis of different forms, each with its own significance. The base is square and represents the earth. The apex is the starting-point and finishing-point of all things—the mystic "Centre." . . . Joining the apex to the base are the triangular-shaped faces of the pyramid, symbolizing fire, divine revelation and the three-fold principle of creation. In consequence, the pyramid is seen as a symbol expressing the whole of creation in its three essential aspects.[79]

Do these mystical proportions place the division of forms in nature under the aegis of the Great Zero (apex) in such a way as to form a perfect precinct of protection? Is this the concretization of Simon Iff-Crowley's formula for magical protection as quoted earlier? It appears that a blunted razor blade left within such a pyramid regains its sharpness. It has been claimed that vegetables freshen and hard fruit ripens in the same way. An American investigator, Patrick Flanagan, suggests that the pyramid acts as a kind of lens for energy produced by the earth's magnetic field. All that one can say is that such an enigma is more easily apprehended by the mind of a Blavatsky than by processes of inductive research.

Certainly, it would seem that Helena Blavatsky was not untouched by fraudulence. It may be that her mind tended to obscure the frontiers of theater and life. But this in itself makes her most unlikely conceptual bonds with such as Kandinsky and Mondrian all the more intriguing. They were not interested in her alleged ability to induce rose petals to fall from the ceiling. They were interested in her insight into noncausal possibility, into a noninductive universe, into reinterpretations of form, and this she was able to offer. There is a steadier, firmer thread to Crowley's story. But hers is scarcely less obsessive in its magnetic force. The fascination of Blavatsky's case is that she is preeminently the sitting duck every rationalist wants a square chance of shattering. She is almost too easy, given her theatrical, shady character. The point, however, is that magic is encapsulated in a variety of strange vessels of eccentric shape. It may be an Artaud, a Crowley or a Blavatsky, but in each case the power evoked is a power beyond the ego, larger than any one medium.

The intellectual association of Mondrian and Blavatsky is bizarre and almost comic: this huge burbling samovar of a Russian woman and the finely chiseled ascetic Dutchman. The lines of force she generated were all voluminous and turbulent, out of the emotional heights and depths of Russian theater; whereas Mondrian's "purist" vocabulary was angular, poised, intellectual, cool of temper, the fitting descendant of Vermeer's world of stasis and light.

He identified his art, which others tended to see merely as abstraction, with a numinous quality. In *De Stijl*, he pronounced the canon that "To denaturalize is to deepen." And he explained his ideal of

. . . a new aesthetic based on pure relationships of lines and pure colours because only the pure relationships of pure constructive elements can achieve a pure beauty. Today, pure beauty is not only a necessity for us, it is the only means to a pure manifestation of the universal force that is in everything. It is identical to what was known in the past under the name of divinity.[80]

One immediately comes to the connection between this thinking eye and the writings of a woman who saw the proportions of the pyramids as the key to active magic. Mondrian banished curved lines and the color green from his work as symbols of nature. At first, an apparent objection may occur: Is not blue as much a color of nature as green? But the answer is that Mondrian had revived a living and truly medieval sense of color symbolism. For the illuminators of Byzantium and of the Middle Ages, blue was very much a divine color under the sign of the Moon, the key to the light of the stained-glass windows of Chartres. Green was the color of nature, or of the life-fluid manifest in terrestrial forms. The so-called primitives did not paint the poplar or the vine green because it happened to be optically so, but because such was its cosmic sigil under the sign of Venus.

The same impetus to unspoken truths led Kandinsky along a path that produced the first truly nonobjective paintings in the history of modern art (Fig. 128). He too was drawn to Theosophy, as well as to the Thought-Forms of Besant

128. Wassily Kandinsky, *Picture with Three Spots #196*, 1914. Oil on canvas. Private collection?

and Leadbeater, two disciples drawn into the magnetic range of the irrepressible Blavatsky. Besant was a reluctant observer who later became the leader of the society; Leadbeater was a fellow whose interest in young boys outranged his involvement in the occult. Both, however, found a strangely new clarity under the aegis of Helena Petrovna Blavatsky. Their Thought-Forms were sufficient to electrify the imagination of two of modern art's most original personalities, men of plastic intent who had no time for random mysticism or obfuscation.

Besant and Leadbeater wrote about light and color as manifestations of spirit. This was light as pure energy and pure soul, much akin to the occult concept of the etheric and astral bodies capable of existing apart from the physical body for short spaces of time in this world and long periods after the body's demise. This color theory had its antecedents in Goethe, whose study of color also recognized a more than symbolic heraldry of mind. Kandinsky's particular rapport with Theosophy happened to be more explicit and more passionate than Mondrian's. The latter drew away eventually, apparently disenchanted with some of the dogma and some of the paraphernalia. Yet both listened intently and found sustenance for two of the most original breakthroughs in modern art.

In 1918 Mondrian wrote:

A true conception of the essential *meaning* of spirit and nature in man shows life and art as a perpetual sacrifice of inward to outward and outward to inward; a conception which enables us to recognize this process as exclusively in favour of the inward and *serving to broaden man's individual inwardness (spirit) toward universal inwardness.* . . . Thus understood, the opposition of spirit and nature in man is seen as constantly forming a *new unity*—which *constantly reflects more purely* the original unity out of which the opposites, spirit and nature, manifest themselves—in time as a duality.[81]

By now this theme is thoroughly familiar as an occult canon or, rather, as an occult striving—like the *natural* striving of a flower that seeks the light with all the thrust and equilibrium of its organism. A fascinating parallel characteristic is the incessant process of physical travel that accompanies this will. Antonello zigzags to Venice by way of the Lowlands and ignites a new illumination. El Greco works an alchemy of Spanish light by way of Venice, after Crete. Picasso leaves Spain to concatenate with Paris. Mondrian leaves Holland for France, is reborn, and consummates his career in New York where the lights of *Broadway Boogie-Woogie* (Fig. 129) fulfill a vision engendered along Vermeer's canals. A Crowley, an Artaud, a Blavatsky, crisscross the globe in insatiable and untiring pursuit of the inner and outer light that radiates anywhere and everywhere. These peregrinations are far more than physical. In part they constitute a commingling of light, for each place has its aura and its vibration just as each individual does. Otherwise the motivation is

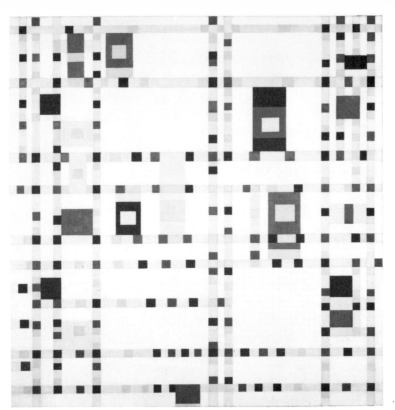

129. Piet Mondrian, *Broadway Boogie-Woogie*, 1942–43. Oil on canvas, 50″ x 50″. Collection, The Museum of Modern Art, N.Y.; anonymous gift.

130. Paul Gauguin, *The Vision after the Sermon*, 1888. Oil on canvas. National Gallery of Scotland, Edinburgh. Annan Photographer, Glasgow.

entirely inner. One associates Paul Gauguin with Tahiti. Yet Gauguin had already found his mysticism at Pont-Aven in Brittany where he evoked Jacob and the Angel (Fig. 130) wrestling before a congregation of Breton women. The exotic influence of the South Seas added less to his power as a painter than has usually been suggested. What it did do was to renew his eye, his mystical vocabulary, in another light; it set his European optic at a new level of disassociation.

In other words, the seeker after illumination tends to be driven outwardly as inwardly along a course of psychic and physical fatality. As he purifies his message, that message often tends to be ever less understood or accepted. The more he wins his vision the more he belongs to it. Movement leads to stasis. Free will leads to a priestly servitude. And this is the sense of still another complex trump in the Tarot, arc. XII, the *Hanged Man* (Fig. 131).

131. Tarot: Arc. XII, *Le Pendu* (The Hanged Man). Woodcut, French, 1760.

132. Tarot: Arc. XI, *La Force* (Strength). Woodcut, French, 1760.

133. Tarot: Arc. XIII, *La Mort* (Death). Woodcut, French, 1760.

Wirth sees this card in terms of *"the disengaged soul enveloping the body"* and of *redemptive sacrifice.* It is the sacrifice of the limited self before higher powers. Crowley chose to see the card not at all as sacrifice but as redemption through a total devotion of Nietzschean will. In either case, however, the self ceases to be self and becomes other. The Hanged Man smiles or gazes with equanimity upon his gibbet. The coins that fall from his pockets in certain packs have been interpreted variously as an indifference to worldly wealth or as the generous dissemination of priceless gifts of knowledge. The legs are crossed in the sign of the Hebrew *Tau,* a cross symbolic of the four elements, earth, air, fire, and water. Note that the same configuration applies to arc. XXI, the Universe; halfway through the Great Wheel the adept has reached a point of stillness in microcosm to the final apotheosis of the last trump. A Tarot scholar, Fred Gettings, comments that the rectangular enclosure in which the Hanged Man is suspended might be associated with the dimension of *Akashya* as defined by Pythagoras: the four walls would again be symbolic of the four elements, while the space within bespeaks the fifth, invisible element—the unseen life-force. The idea of the precinct reemerges here as a meeting of labyrinth and void. And it may be that this perspective had something to do with the little girl's dream of "God coming from the four corners."

In magic and in poetry this trump bespeaks a difficult and precarious position. The helpless devotee is situated between arc. XI, Strength (Fig. 132), and arc. XIII, the Death Card (Fig. 133). The former shows a blonde girl subduing a lion, not by physical force but by virtue of intelligence or will. She is the female incarnation of the magical, noninductive luminous will, and, like the Magician's, her hat forms the sign of Infinity. On the other side, the Death Card takes the element of sacrifice into a new dimension. It speaks of death as rebirth in a sense parallel to that of the Hindu Siva. It is through the grace of having mastered Strength that the adept of the Hanged Man may pass reborn through the grim process of the Death Card. But woe to him who enters here without sufficient preparation and protection. If he succeeds, however, he meets with the heightened consciousness of equilibrium and time embodied in arc. XIV, Temperance. We discussed this trump earlier in connection with the hermaphroditic Devil, the male-female duality, the solar-lunar connection. Now it assumes further meaning. Speaking of this presence, which is either of dual sex or beyond sex entirely, Wirth commented on the universal fluid that passes endlessly between the golden-solar urn and its silver-lunar counterpart. He saw this flow as "The universal Life . . . the restoring and reconstituting agent of all that wears down and declines. The medicinal energy of Nature . . . Transfusion of vital strength, curative magnetism, occult or mystical medicine. . . ."[82]

After this, it seems brilliantly appropriate that Crowley chose to call this key not Temperance but Art! For this is the point along the Great Wheel at which art becomes possible. The psychic is joined with the concrete as reason and perception form an equation of energy.

Significantly, what we have here is also a balance and even an identity of time and timelessness. This explains a great paradox in the artist's task: that he must always work within his time in order to be timeless; that he is always a spokesman of his time while becoming so universal in expression as to speak vividly to all times. If he falls short in the vivification of the vital current his work appears dated—he sinks into the relativity of approximate time. If he succeeds his work becomes eternal, archetypal, alive, and always modern. This is why the chronological approach to art history is so often lacking. The story of Renaissance art, for example, is usually related as a progression from "primitive" vision through a growing humanism and physical sophistication. Giotto paints the sky blue rather than gold, and begins to introduce elements of optically true perspective. Then, through Masaccio and Piero in Tuscany, through Bellini and Mantegna in Venice, the process intensifies until it reaches the fleshly perfections of Michelangelo and Raphael. Yet this is only half the story at best, since it is the temporal story. For if the same "progression" is seen against the grain of time—backwards—its occult or timeless quality becomes immediately more visible: Raphael tries to express the madonna, but can do so only through the physical presence, through the outer shell, through *matter*. Just as El Greco felt that there was too much meat in Michelangelo's heaven; he found the astral light too heavily masked. Whereupon the means are gradually developed towards a purer, more internal vision. The eye acclimates to other lights until Giotto at last creates a new wavelength and begins to flatten out optical perspective in favor of a frieze apprehended by the inner eye. With the so-called "primitives" the husk of outer reality is at last minimized; the sky turns to gold.

Time-Future

It may well be that time—a vast and never wholly graspable subject—is the key to perception. Max Planck saw it as the arbiter of light, and hence of all perceptual reality. Marcel Proust sensed its close-to-tangible presence as the medium of experience. As noted earlier the *speed* of light would seem to describe the most exclusive perimeter of our bodily possibilities. The two great protosurrealists, Chirico and Chagall, were acutely attuned to time—Chagall who applied the title *Half-Past Three* (Fig. 134) to a vision of the dream-eternity, and whose flying clocks waft through timelessness; Chirico whose clocks stare glumly out of vast solitudes beyond time (Fig. 135). In *Persistence of Memory* (Fig. 136), Dali paints time fading back, dissolving into the "sensitive chaos" of primal flux, a process which he described as "psychic anamorphism."

One notes that as material "progress" accelerates, we increasingly become the plaything of time. While the average life span has doubled, and while technology yields larger periods of leisure, there is *time* for less and less. Suddenly, "time flies" mysteriously in an age when men fly faster than the speed of sound. The machine beats time as upon the kettle drum of a Roman galley, and we slave to its rhythm. Fashion supplants art as the psyche struggles helplessly toward the immediate, against some invisible tide. Trends succeed trends with ever greater celerity. The present becomes a frustrating obsession while, conversely, successive tides of "nostalgia" well up—as though timelessness and its magic might be locatable in fragments of the past. Finally, the specter of global annihilation looms up as perhaps the only species of timelessness within our means—an end to time, from our mortal point of view.

134. Marc Chagall, *Half-Past Three*, 1911. Oil on canvas. Philadelphia Museum of Art, Louise and Walter Arensberg Collection.

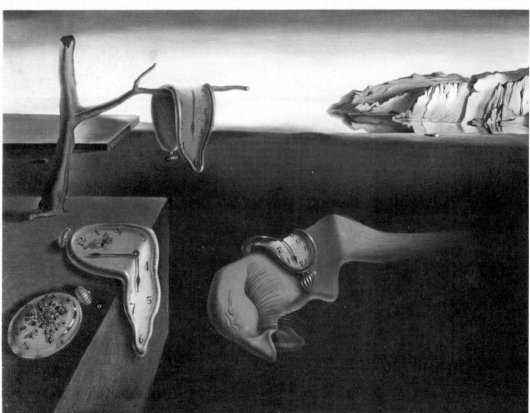

135. Giorgio de Chirico, *The Delights of the Poet*, 1913. Oil on canvas, 27⅜″ x 34″. Collection Leonard C. Yaseen.

136. Salvador Dali, *Persistence of Memory*, 1931. Oil on canvas. 9½″ x 13″. Collection, The Museum of Modern Art, N.Y. Given anonymously.

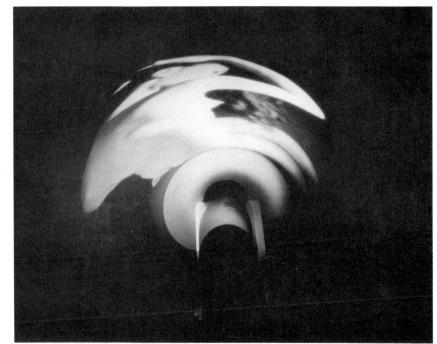

137. Nude Figure. Photo Alan Fontaine.

138. Nude Figure. Photo Alan Fontaine.

That point of view can distort and destroy as well as create, and can reconstruct its own distortions into new harmonies. An anamorphic image is one that has been distended along a curve until it becomes an indecipherable code which, however, can be reconstituted when mirrored against a curved cylinder. The nude (Figs. 137, 138) becomes a cosmic circle in its anamorphic form, only to become organically female again when so reflected. Such a technique goes back to Van Eyck and Quentin Matsys, and to Holbein; but the technique is less important than the idea. Martin Gardner quotes Thomas Jefferson's words on men and God: "It was to correct their anamorphosis of the Deity that Jesus preached." [83] And it is to correct the anamorphosis of materialist and mechanical presumption that occult vision is now dedicated.

The fact that formal education has not taken the cue may be tragic—or it may be a blessing. Blake thundered, "There is no use in education. . . . I hold it wrong—it is the great Sin." [84] He saw it as the deformation of the mind. Over a century later, George Bernard Shaw declared that the shaping of a child's mind is the worst form of abortion. So it may be all the better that occult illumination is a precious power to be ferreted out of the darkness rather than a dose administered in flat daylight. In that way it is closer to love than to learning—though it is both—and it retains a more awesome brilliance.

Visibly, the art movements of the present tend toward an occult orientation. "Minimal" art concerns itself with a pure "division of space" in painting and sculpture, and "conceptual" art seeks to be a servant of mind in which the actual object—a pile of stones, a rope, a vacant light effect—counts for nothing in its material self. The great problem here, however, is that the result is usually neither minimal enough nor conceptual enough. The material presence remains material, the presentation remains formal, and the association with the creative impulse of a given artist remains a connection with the romantic tradition as well as with the first-person singular. The attempt vacillates in mid psychic stream. There is neither the assertion nor conflagration of the self implicit in a Van Gogh or a Cézanne, nor the priestly anonymity of the sculptors of Chartres or the architects of Ghiza. It is a reaching out, a troubled response, a mottled hope.

Yet "conceptual art" may well be the way of the future. It remains for the tendency to become entirely conceptual, to link up—again—with the processes of magic.

What is certain is that time is flexible at best and illusory at worst, and that the poet-magician of the future will abide harmoniously, beyond time, with his counterparts of the past. He too will be a student of the light and a servant of the Law. He will proclaim not a revolution but a mystical continuity. He will not announce the coming of his own self-expression, but will manifest his genius in the harmony of a higher power. His humility will be astonished at the prowess it generates. He will at first walk with the amazement of a child through a world that is stunningly new and luminous and fraught with possibility. The equation will be new and the same, transformed into another modernity in an unrecognizable age.

Appendix: The Tarot

The Magician, key to the initial creative force in man, is followed by *The High Priestess* who transmutes this will into a form of pure thought, and then by *The Empress* who concretizes that thought into a manifest, intellectual work. These cards have been likened to the first three Euclidian expressions: the point, the straight line, and the two-dimensional plane. *The Emperor* then takes the sequence a step further into a worldly solidity, as symbolized by the cube. This temporal state, however, is immediately arbitrated by Mind and Law in the presence of *The Pope* or *Hierophant*. At this crucial juncture, *The Lovers* introduces human choice between higher and lower expressions of creative power. Whereupon *The Chariot* represents a driving force capable of containing and directing disparate energies. *Justice* follows reasserting the elements of balance, reflection, and legitimacy; succeeded by *The Hermit* who embodies an intensity of inner vision and searching evaluation. Now the individual is better equipped to encounter *The Wheel of Fortune* in its cyclical revolutions through vicissitude and triumph. After which, *Strength* implies the power of will, of mind, of art and magic, over circumstance.

As discussed in the text, the adept learns the rich serenity and resignation of *The Hanged Man*, passes through the necessary transmutation of *Death*, and encounters the magical harmony or balance of *Temperance*. He is then better prepared to confront the enigma of *The Devil* and to survive the menace of *The Tower*. If he does so, he arrives at *The Star*, a happy symbol of enlightenment and of hope. He is now ready to transverse the perils of *The Moon* and to welcome the generative and sustaining brilliance of *The Sun*; then to pass through the redemption of *Judgement* into the apotheosis of *The World* or *Universe* in which the Great Zero is reconstituted.

In the Great Circle of Tarota (Fig. a), the Zero card, *The Fool*, is neither the beginning nor the end, but both. However, when the keys are arranged according to Fig. b—which can be taken as a hermetically anamorphic reconstitution of the Circle, much like a mercator projection of the globe as a flat map—still other relationships come to light. *The Fool* and *The Magician* are twinned; as above, so below. *The Wheel of Fortune* mirrors the cyclical implications of *Death*. The question of choice in *The Lovers* is reflected by the miasmic searchings of *The Moon*. In addition, the arcana can now be analyzed according to ternary and quaternary suits. And finally, when the pack is used for divination, all suits and juxtapositions of cards will be seen by the adept to comment on an individual's past, present, and future in respect to the creative force, to the world. For the Tarot crystallizes light, energy, or spirit just as a kaleidoscope draws fragments of shape and color into successive harmonic patterns. It must be added, however, that no manual or book is sufficient to teach divination through the Tarot. This ability comes through a process of study, knowledge, experience, and finally of instinctive sympathy, as complex as the study of life itself.

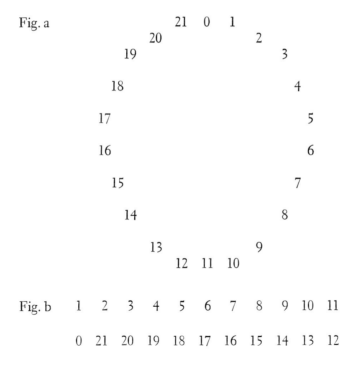

Fig. a

```
                          21  0  1
                    20                 2
                 19                        3
               18                            4
               17                              5
               16                              6
                15                            7
                 14                        8
                   13                 9
                     12  11  10
```

Fig. b   1   2   3   4   5   6   7   8   9   10   11

          0   21 20 19 18 17 16 15 14 13 12

See overleaf for the major
keys of the Tarot.

1. William Blake, "Auguries of Innocence." See Bibliography.
2. Loren Eiseley, *The Unexpected Universe*. New York: Harcourt Brace Jovanovich, 1964, pp. 49–50.
3. William Blake, "The Marriage of Heaven and Hell."
4. Henry Adams, "The Dynamo and the Virgin," in *The Education of Henry Adams*, 1973.
5. Arthur Koestler, *The Roots of Coincidence*. London: Hutchinson, 1972, p. 99.
6. Eiseley, op. cit., p. 88.
7. Henry David Thoreau, *The Journal of Henry David Thoreau*, ed. Bradford Torrey & Francis H. Allen. Boston: Houghton Mifflin, 1949.
8. Jean Cocteau, "Le Potomak," in *Cocteau's World*, ed. Margaret Crosland. London: Peter Owen, 1972, p. 95.
9. Paul Klee, *The Diaries of Paul Klee, 1898–1918*, ed. Felix Klee. Berkeley: University of California Press, 1964.
10. Theodor Schwenk, *Sensitive Chaos*. London: Rudolph Steiner Press, 1965, p. 13.
11. Oswald Wirth, *Le Tarot et les imagiers du moyen age*. Paris: Tchou, 1966, p. 255.
12. Aleister Crowley, *The Book of Thoth*, p. 53. See Bibliography.
13. T. S. Eliot, "Little Gidding," in *Four Quartets*. London: Faber & Faber, 1944, p. 59.
14. William Hazlitt, quoted in *The Romantic Rebellion: Romantic vs. Classic Art*, by Kenneth Clark. London: John Murray and Sotheby-Parke Bernet, 1973, p. 259.
15. Wirth, op. cit., pp. 201–202.
16. Crowley, op. cit., p. 107.
17. Wirth, op. cit., p. 203.
18. William Blake, "The Tyger," in *Songs of Experience*, 1794.
19. J. E. Cirlot, *A Dictionary of Symbols*. London: Routledge & Kegan Paul, 1971, p. 247.
20. Heraclitus, *On Nature*.
21. Louis Pasteur, in *Dictionary of Science*, eds. E. B. Uvarov and D. R. Chapman. London: Penguin, 1943, p. 282.
22. Duc de la Rouchefoucauld, *Maximes*.
23. Carlos Castaneda, *A Separate Reality*, p. 154. See Bibliography.
24. Jean Cocteau, *Beauty Secrets*, quoted in Crosland, ed., op. cit., p. 475.
25. Alfred North Whitehead, quoted in *The Roots of Coincidence* by Arthur Koestler. London: Hutchinson, p. 110.
26. Aldous Huxley, *The Doors of Perception*. London: Penguin, 1954.
27. Paul Klee, *Paul Klee on Modern Art*. London: Faber & Faber, 1948, p. 15.
28. Herman Melville, *Moby Dick*.
29. Jorge Luis Borges, *Fictions*, p. 59. See Bibliography.
30. Thomas De Quincey, *Confessions of an English Opium Eater*.
31. C. G. Jung, *Man and His Symbols*, p. 70. See Bibliography.
32. J. E. Cirlot, op. cit., p. 263.
33. Antonin Artaud, letter of June 5, 1923, trans. Bernard Frechtman,

in *Artaud Anthology*, ed. Jack Hirschman. San Francisco: City Lights Books, 1965.

34. Artaud, "An Actor You Can See . . . ," trans. Marc Estrin, in *Artaud Anthology*, pp. 34–35.
35. Artaud, "It is the Act Which Shapes Our Thought . . . ," trans. Raymond Federman, in *Artaud Anthology*, p. 29.
36. Antonin Artaud, *Les Tarahumaras*, p. 44. See Bibliography. Author's translation.
37. Ibid., pp. 56–57.
38. Castaneda, op. cit., p. 111.
39. André Breton, quoted in *Miró*, by Jacques Lassaigne. Geneva: Skira, 1963, p. 35.
40. Antonin Artaud, *Oeuvres Complètes*, vol. XIII, *Van Gogh, le suicidé de la société*. Paris: Gallimard, 1974, p. 15.
41. Ibid. *Post-Scriptum*, p. 20.
42. Jean Cocteau, *The Myth of El Greco*, in op. cit., p. 261.
43. William Rubin, *Miró in the Collection of the Museum of Modern Art*. New York: Museum of Modern Art, 1973, p. 76.
44. Francisco Goya, quoted in Kenneth Clark, op. cit., p. 95.
45. Friedrich Nietzsche, *Twilight of the Gods (Maxims and Arrows)*. London: Penguin, 1968, p. 27.
46. John Symonds, *The Great Beast: The Life and Magick of Aleister Crowley*. London: Mayflower, 1973, p. 37.
47. Nietzsche, op. cit., p. 25.
48. Crowley, op. cit., p. 243.
49. Symonds, op. cit., p. 228.
50. Ibid.
51. Nietzsche, op. cit., p. 23.
52. Aleister Crowley, *Moonchild*, p. 72. See Bibliography.
53. Aleister Crowley, *The Confessions of Aleister Crowley*, pp. 351–352. See Bibliography.
54. Ibid., p. 879.
55. D. H. Lawrence, "Kissing and Horrid Strife," from *Last Poems*, 1929. In *Selected Poems*, London: Penguin, 1972, p. 249.
56. D. H. Lawrence, "Retort to Jesus," *Nettles and More Pansies*, 1929. In Ibid., p. 225.
57. Max Ernst, quoted in *The Essential Max Ernst* by Uwe M. Schneede. New York: Praeger (World of Art Library), 1972, p. 21.
58. Ibid., p. 23.
59. Wirth, op. cit., p. 194.
60. W. B. Yeats, quoted in Yeats, *The Tarot and the Golden Dawn* by Kathleen Raine, p. 52. See Bibliography.
61. W. B. Yeats, "Meditation in Time of War," *Selected Poems*. London: Penguin, p. 112.
62. Michael Holroyd, *Augustus John*, Vol. I, *Years of Innocence*. London: Heinemann, 1974, p. 124.
63. James Cleugh, *Oriental Orgies*. London: Anthony Blond, 1968, p. 132.
64. Philip Rawson, *Tantra: The Indian Cult of Ecstasy*. London: Thames & Hudson, 1974, pp. 16–17.

65. Ibid., p. 15.
66. *New LaRousse Encyclopaedia of Mythology* (1959). London: Hamlyn, 1973, p. 132.
67. Percy Bysshe Shelley, "Adonais: Elegy on the Death of John Keats."
68. John Keats, "On Seeing the Elgin Marbles."
69. Hermann Hesse, *Siddhartha.* See Bibliography.
70. Jean Cocteau, *Cock and Harlequin,* quoted in *Cocteau's World,* op. cit., p. 311.
71. Jean Cocteau, *The Myth of El Greco,* quoted op. cit., p. 266.
72. Maurice Nadeau, *The History of Surrealism* (1964). London: Pelican Books, 1973, p. 167.
73. Edward Russell, *Design for Destiny.* London: Nevile Spearman, 1971.
74. Werner Heisenberg, "Science: The Tradition: End of an Epoch?", *Encounter,* March, 1975, p. 36.
75. Colin Wilson, *The Occult.* London: Hodder & Stoughton, 1971, p. 336.
76. Ibid., p. 330.
77. *International Herald Tribune,* December 7, 1974.
78. Lyall Watson, *Supernature.* New York: Coronet, 1974, p. 100.
79. J. E. Cirlot, op. cit., p. 351.
80. Piet Mondrian, quoted in *Cubism* by Paul Waldo-Schwartz. New York: Praeger (World of Art Library), 1971, p. 193.
81. Piet Mondrian, *De Stijl* (June, 1918). Quoted in *Mondrian* by Hans L. C. Jaffe. London: Thames & Hudson (World of Art Library), 1970, p. 68.
82. Oswald Wirth, op. cit., pp. 197–198.
83. Martin Gardner, "The Curious Magic of Anamorphic Art," *Scientific American,* January, 1975, p. 116.
84. Kathleen Raine, *William Blake,* op. cit., p. 11.

Selected Bibliography

An introductory key to the sense and substance of the occult in art

General

ARTAUD, ANTONIN, *Van Gogh le Suicidé de la Société, Oeuvres Complètes*, vol XIII. Paris: Gallimard, 1974, pp. 13 ff.

————, *Les Tarahumaras*. Paris: Gallimard, 1971.

BLAKE, WILLIAM, *The Complete Writings of William Blake.* Ed. G. Keynes. New York: Oxford University Press, 1966.

CASTANEDA, CARLOS, *A Separate Reality*. London: Penguin Books, 1973.

CIRLOT, J. E., *A Dictionary of Symbols*. London: Routledge & Kegan Paul, 1971.

EISELEY, LOREN, *The Unexpected Universe*. New York: Harcourt Brace Jovanovich, 1964.

HAYNES, RENEE, *The Hidden Springs: An enquiry into extra-sensory perception*. London: Hutchinson, 1961.

HUXLEY, ALDOUS, *The Doors of Perception* and *Heaven and Hell*. London: Penguin Books, 1959.

JUNG, C. G., *Man and His Symbols*. London: Aldus Books, 1972.

————, *The Spirit in Man, Art and Literature* (*The Collected Works*, Vol. xv). London: Routledge & Kegan Paul, 1971.

KOESTLER, ARTHUR, *The Roots of Coincidence*. London: Hutchinson, 1972.

PEARCE, JOSEPH CHILTON, *The Crack in the Cosmic Egg*. New York: Pocket Books, 1973.

RAINE, KATHLEEN, *William Blake*. London: Thames & Hudson (World of Art Library); New York: Praeger, 1970.

————, *Yeats, the Tarot and the Golden Dawn*. Dublin: The Dolmen Press, 1972.

SCHWENK, THEODOR, *Sensitive Chaos*. London: Rudolph Steiner Press, 1965.

TenHOUTEN, WARREN D., and KAPLAN, CHARLES D., *Science and Its Mirror Image*. New York and London: Harper & Row, 1973.

Occult

BESANT, ANNIE, and LEADBEATER, C. W., *Thought-Forms*.

Wheaton, Ill.: The Theosophical Classics Series, 1901; London: Madras, 1971.

BLAVATSKY, H. P., *Studies in Occultism*. Pasadena: Theosophical University Press, no date.

CROWLEY, ALEISTER, *The Confessions of Aleister Crowley*. Eds. John Symonds and Kenneth Grant. New York: Bantam, 1971.

————, *The Book of Thoth (Egyptian Tarot)*, 1944. New York: Samuel Weiser, Inc., 1972.

PURCE, JILL, *The Mystic Spiral; Journey of the Soul*. London: Thames & Hudson, 1974.

RAWSON, PHILIP, *Tantra: The Indian Cult of Ecstasy*. London: Thames & Hudson, 1974.

WILSON, COLIN, *The Occult*. London: Hodder and Stoughton, 1971.

WIRTH, OSWALD, *Le Tarot des imagiers du moyen age*. Paris: Tchou, 1966.

Fiction

BORGES, JORGE LUIS, *Fictions* (1962). London: John Calder, 1965.

CROWLEY, ALEISTER, *Moonchild* (1929). New York: Mandrake, 1972.

HESSE, HERMANN, *Siddhartha*.

LAWRENCE, D. H., "The Man Who Died," included in *Love Among the Haystacks and Other Stories*. London: Penguin Books, 1974.

MEYRINK, GUSTAV, *The Golem*. Prague & San Francisco: Mudra, 1972.